THE MIND OF TENNYSON

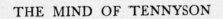

The
Mind of Tennyson

HIS THOUGHTS ON GOD, FREEDOM,
AND IMMORTALITY

BY

E. HERSHEY SNEATH, Ph.D.

PROFESSOR OF PHILOSOPHY IN YALE UNIVERSITY

"We have but faith: we cannot know"

NEW YORK
CHARLES SCRIBNER'S SONS
1901

UNIVERSITY PRESS · JOHN WILSON
AND SON · CAMBRIDGE, U.S.A.

TO

MY FATHER AND MOTHER

PREFACE

THE aim of this little book is to interpret and systematise Tennyson's thoughts on God, Freedom, and Immortality. Great care has been taken not to force the interpretation in any manner, but to determine as nearly as possible just what the poet thought on these "inevitable questions." To this end special effort has been made to distinguish between the subjective and objective, — the personal and impersonal, — in his poetry; also, to make due allowance for metaphor and poetic license. The interpretation has, of course, been made in the light of Tennyson's relation to the spirit of his age.

Tennyson was such a consummate artist that a large number of his readers are, very naturally, more interested in the form than in the substance of his poetry. He was, however, a poet with "a conscience and an aim," and the aim was primarily an ethical one. He had something to say which he deemed to be of vital import in its bearing on human life and conduct. Therefore, a knowledge of his " message " is necessary to an adequate understanding and appreciation of both the poet and his art, — whatever of value we may attribute to the message itself. That this little book will contribute to this end, is the earnest hope of the author.

E. H. S.

CONTENTS

THE

MIND OF TENNYSON

INTRODUCTION

The truths that never can be proved.
In Memoriam, cxxxi., 3.

The faith, the vigour, bold to dwell
On doubts that drive the coward back.
In Memoriam, xcv., 8.

TENNYSON, throughout the greater
part of his life, was greatly interested in the problems of philosophy.
They constituted one of the main sources
of his poetical inspiration, and occupy
a conspicuous place in the productions
of his genius. Early in his career as
a poet, we find him engaged in a con-
test with scepticism concerning them.
This is manifest in the poem entitled,
*Supposed Confessions of a Second-Rate Sen-
sitive Mind.* A little later, in *The Two*

Voices, he considers the problem of the worth of human life.   Again, in *The Palace of Art*, he reflects upon important aspects of moral life and theory.   In the *Higher Pantheism*, he treats of the ultimate nature of reality, and of the relation of the finite to the Infinite — two of the most fundamental problems of metaphysics.   In *In Memoriam*, he meditates long and seriously upon the great problems of God and immortality; upon the mysterious realities of sin and suffering; upon the problems of knowledge, — its origin, nature, reality, development, extent; its distinction from faith, — almost unconsciously constructing a kind of philosophy of life.   In the *Idylls of the King*, the

> "old imperfect tale,
> New-old, and shadowing Sense at war with Soul,"

"the spiritually central lines" concern the reality of God, the finite spirit, and immortality.   In *De Profundis*, we have thoughts upon the mystery of birth, in

which he hints at the pre-existence of
the soul; and also upon the mystery of
personality, —

> "this main-miracle, that thou art thou,
> With power on thine own act and on the world."

In *The Ancient Sage*, he opposes materialistic and agnostic views of God and
immortality, and presents suggestions
concerning the value of proof in the
domain of fundamentals, — pointing out
the limits of proof, and the province and
value of faith. In *Despair*, he reveals his
knowledge and opinions of a cold and
heartless theology on the one hand, and
an atheistic and agnostic philosophy on
the other, — of the severe creeds of the
"know-all chapel," and the "horrible infidel writings," or "know-nothing books,"
of "the new dark ages." In *The Promise
of May*, he strikes at some of the prominent philosophical tendencies of the age
as they bear upon human conduct. In
Vastness, the subject of immortality is

again under consideration.   Finally, in poems like those entitled, *By an Evolutionist*, *The Dawn*, and *The Making of Man*, he reflects upon the ultimate goal of man's evolution.   Thus we see, that almost from the beginning to the end of his poetical career, Tennyson was earnestly interested in, and concerned with, the deeper and profounder problems of the human mind.

Nor are we dependent upon internal evidence alone to convince us of the truth of this statement.   There is a large amount of external evidence which establishes it beyond a doubt.   In the *Memoir*,[1] recently published by Hallam Lord Tennyson, we are told that a group of friends, of which Tennyson was one, who constituted the "Apostles'" club, of Cambridge, during his university career, "read their Hobbes, Locke, Berkeley, Butler, Hume, Bentham, Descartes, and Kant, and discussed such questions as the Origin of

[1] Alfred Lord Tennyson: A Memoir by his Son. New York, 1897.   Vol. i., pp. 43, 44.

Evil, the Derivation of Moral Sentiments, Prayer, and the Personality of
God." We are further informed, that
"soon after his marriage he took to reading different systems of philosophy," and
that "Spinoza, Berkeley, Kant, Schlegel,
Fichte, Hegel, Ferrier, were among the
books added to his library."[1] Again, we
learn, that he was one of the founders of
the Metaphysical Society of Great Brit-
ain, established for the discussion of fundamental questions of the Christian faith.
It was composed of adherents and oppo-
nents of the Faith. Among its members
were such distinguished philosophical
thinkers as Martineau, Hodgson, Sidg-
wick, Fraser, and Croom Robertson; such
prominent biblical and theological schol-
ars as Maurice, Stanley, Mozley, and
Alford; such notable men of science as
Huxley, Tyndall, Sir John Lubbock, and
St. George Mivart; such renowned men
of letters as Tennyson, Hutton, Ruskin,

[1] Memoir, vol. i., p. 308.

and Froude.[1] Dr. Martineau tells us, that some of the subjects discussed in the meetings when Tennyson was present were, "The Common-sense Philosophy of Causation," "Is there any Axiom of Causation?" "The Relativity of Knowledge," "The Emotion of Conviction," "What is Death?" "The Supposed Necessity for Seeking a Solution of Ultimate Metaphysical Problems," "The Five Idols of the Theatre," "Utilitarianism," and "Double Truth."[2] Again, in his letter-diary, we find, under date of Dec. 14, 1865, that he had called on Tyndall "and had a long chat with him about mind and matter, etc."[3] In Lady Tennyson's Journal, under date of August 17, 1866, she writes that "A. [Alfred] and Edmund [Lushington] talked metaphysics. They have engrossed A. much of late."[4] Tennyson's son informs us, that "the philosophers of

1 Memoir, vol. ii., pp. 166, 167.
2 Ibid., pp. 170, 171.
3 Ibid., p. 32.
4 Ibid., p. 39.

the East had a great fascination " for his father.[1] *Akbar's Dream* is a testimony to this fact. Finally, Locker-Lampson, Lecky, Jowett, Tyndall, and the Duke of Argyll, in their contributions to the *Memoir*, all bear witness to Tennyson's great interest in the questions of speculative thought.

The causes of this peculiar interest in the problems of philosophy are not difficult to determine. In the first place, it was due, in a measure, to poetic temperament. The poet is essentially a man of reflection, and this at once puts him in touch with the almost permanent mood of the philosopher; and very naturally leads him to the subject-matter of philosophy. Again, the æsthetic nature is one of the main sources of philosophy itself. It has its ideals of the beautiful and sublime, and posits an objective reality as their Ground. In its more refined and profound moods the æsthetic nature is led on to the recog·

[1] Memoir, vol. ii., p. 388.

nition of a Supreme Reality, which is the perfect embodiment or realisation of absolute beauty. It is an interesting fact to note, that the ontological argument for the being and nature of God, which argues the existence of a Perfect Being from the necessary Idea of the Perfect within the mind, has, in a measure, its roots in the æsthetic nature of man. It is equally worthy of note, that the teleological argument for the intelligence of the Deity, based on the apparent adaptation of means to ends, order and harmony, beauty and proportion, in the world, has its roots also in the constitutional æstheticism of man. It is not, then, a matter of wonder that poets like Sophocles and Lucretius, Dante and Milton, Shakespeare and Goethe, Wordsworth and Shelley, Browning and Tennyson, have found much in the problems of philosophy to engage their attention and to inspire their genius.

But poetic temperament was not the only cause of Tennyson's interest in

these great questions. Another cause
was his severe struggle with his own
doubts, and with the doubts of his age.
He was not a "born-believer." Constitu-
tionally he was not predisposed to take
things on authority, but rather to inquire

> "into the laws
> Of life and death, and things that seem,
> And things that be, and analyse
> Our double nature, and compare
> All creeds till we have found the one,
> If one there be."

There was a long and bitter struggle with
his own questionings, and a noble endeavor
to get a solid footing with reference to
the "Eternal Verities." This personal
struggle received a tremendous impulse
through the loss of his much-loved friend,
Arthur Henry Hallam. He himself tells
us, —

> "Like Paul with beasts, I fought with Death."

He fought with those doubts which death
usually suggests concerning the reality of
God, and his divine Fatherhood; the

meaning and worth of human life, and
the final destiny of the human spirit.
All through those seventeen years — the
period covered in writing *In Memoriam* —
a soul knowing "its own bitterness,"
wrapped in profound meditation, tried
manfully to beat back its own scepticism
by patient, earnest inquiry into the
rational grounds for believing that God
is; that He is personal; that He is essential Justice and Love; that life, with its
love and duty, has intrinsic worth and
meaning; that destiny is something
loftier than the dust. It was a sublime struggle, and a triumphant outcome, as the prologue to *In Memoriam*
testifies.[1]

Then, too, the age was an age of active
questioning and doubt — and, indeed, in a
large measure, of positive denial. Science
was making tremendous progress, and, as
is more or less characteristic of such

[1] The prologue bears the date 1849. *In Memoriam*
was published 1850.

periods, although not necessarily so,
Materialism attended her advance. The
mechanical conception of the world,
recognising only necessary sequence in
the explanation of phenomena, was conspicuous in scientific and philosophic
thought. This view was supposed by
many to bear strongly against the teleological argument for the intelligence of
the World-Ground, and against the reality
of self-determining spirit.

> " And as of old from Sinai's top
>   God said that God is One,
>   By Science strict so speaks He now
>   To tell us, There is None !
>   Earth goes by chemic forces ; Heaven 's
>   A Mécanique Céleste !
>   And heart and mind of human kind
>   A watch-work as the rest ! " [1]

Again, the theory of the correlation of
forces was almost universally accepted
among students of science, — at least, so
far as it referred to physical and chemical
forces. It did not take long to extend it

[1] Arthur Hugh Clough, *The New Sinai.*

to the domain of life, and it required but one step more to apply it to the psychic realm — the realm of consciousness. This theory, as applied to life and mind, favored Materialism, and very naturally raised serious doubts as to the existence of a Supreme Spirit called God; as to whether men, in the final analysis, are anything more than highly organised matter, or "cunning casts in clay."

Furthermore, the theory of organic evolution was widely accepted in the scientific world. Its claims concerning the origin of species, especially man, were so at variance with previous and contemporary theological opinion that, for a while, they caused grave anxiety in the world of religious thought and belief. Man being so completely a part of Nature, as this theory indicates, and seems to substantiate by exceedingly convincing lines of evidence, what about his relations to the Supernatural? With such an apparently low origin, what about the divine stamp — the image of God — which the Christian world has always supposed him to bear? With such a low ancestry, and therefore such a common nature, how about his claims on immortality? Does not acceptance of this theory, it was asked, compromise the great beliefs on these questions in which the Christian soul has wrought and rested through the ages?

Again, Darwin's explanation of evolution, largely from the standpoint of natural selection, involving a dreadful struggle for existence, delivered a staggering blow to faith in the goodness and love of God. Nature,

> " red in tooth and claw,
> With ravine shriek'd against his creed."

These were some of the questions which the progress of science raised in the minds of thoughtful men. And, indeed, it is not surprising that many minds, resting serenely in an inherited belief, were shaken out of their "dogmatic slumber," only to be plunged into serious doubt and scepticism.

Nor was the trend of philosophical thought in this age more favorable to positive acceptance of the so-called "fundamental truths," but rather against it. Two conspicuous tendencies characterise the philosophy of this period: Sensationalism and Transcendentalism. Sensationalism, on its ontological side, that is, on the side of being, means that, so far as the ultimate nature of the human mind is concerned, it is nothing more than a bundle of sensations.[1] All of man's higher mental activities are ultimately reducible to sensations, grouped according to certain laws of association. Hence man, so far as his psychical being is concerned, is only —

" A willy-nilly current of sensations."

[1] It takes essentially the position which Hume took several centuries ago : "But setting aside some metaphysicians of this kind, I may venture to affirm of the rest of mankind, that they are nothing but a bundle or collection of different perceptions, which succeed each other with an inconceivable rapidity, and are in a perpetual flux and movement." — *A Treatise of Human Nature*, vol. i., pt. iv., sec. vi.

This, of course, cancels the reality of the soul as a distinct, unitary agent or subject of conscious states. In this denial of the reality of mind was involved, as a matter of course, the denial of its freedom and immortality; for, under such circumstances, there is no mind to be free and immortal.

These were the implications of Sensationalism viewed from an ontological standpoint. When we look at it from an epistemological standpoint, that is, from the side of knowledge, the result is equally significant. Its logical implication, as well as its professed position, is Phenomenalism — which means Agnosticism. Knowledge does not extend beyond phenomena. It is limited to things as they appear to us through the senses, and does not reach to reality as it is in itself. The ultimate nature of things cannot be known. What this means with reference to our knowlege of God is, of course, apparent. God is, according to this

theory, "the Unknown and the Unknowable." In short, Sensationalism, on the
side of being, cancels the reality, freedom,
and immortality of finite spirit; and, on
the side of knowing, shuts us out from the
domain of reality — dooming us to a hopeless Agnosticism with reference to Infinite
Spirit.

Nor do we fare any better at the hands
of the more subtle and refined Transcendentalism of the age. This was an inheri-
tance from Kant, through his immortal
work, *The Critique of Pure Reason*. It,
too, is Phenomenalism and Agnosticism
— but of a different character. Kant
held that things are known to us under
the subjective forms of sense-intuition —
space and time. He further held, that
the categories of the understanding, —
cause and effect, subject and attribute,
etc., — which unite our sense-objects, are
also subjective, that is, do not apply
to things-in-themselves. So that we can
only know things as they appear to us

under these forms and categories, and
not as they really are. Furthermore,
not only has sense its native forms, and
understanding its à priori categories, but
reason has its native ideas — the Soul,
the World, and God. Their function or
office is to unify the judgments of the
understanding. They do not apply to
reality — they also are merely subjective.
If we apply them to reality, we fall into
hopeless contradiction. The outcome of
Kant's *Critique* is the destruction of
the foundations of Rational Psychology,
Rational Cosmology, and Rational Theology. Now, this Transcendentalism, involving the most formidable scepticism
in the history of speculative thought,
appeared later, in modified forms, in the
works of some of Tennyson's contemporaries. The depressing and demoralising
effect of such teaching is apparent when
we remember that it shuts out God, the
human soul, and its destiny, from the
knowledge of man by the very constitution

of human knowledge itself. How profoundly Tennyson was affected by these views, will be seen when we examine his teaching on the subjects of God, Freedom, and Immortality.

The religious world, also, was greatly agitated by important movements which had a tendency to shake the confidence of many in the authority of the Scriptures, and the validity of traditional dogma. Quite early in Tennyson's age we have the liberal movement of the early Oriel School. It involved an attack on the infallible authority of the Church and the Sacred Scriptures. Both Archbishop Whately and Thomas Arnold — representatives of this movement — assailed the doctrine of apostolic succession; and the latter denied the dogma of Scriptural inerrancy, anticipating, also, some of the positions of the later so-called "Higher Criticism." On the other hand, we have the celebrated Oxford movement, led by Newman and others, representing an essentially opposite trend. It was a movement in the direction of the infallible authority of the Church, and ultra conceptions and beliefs concerning the saving efficacy of the sacraments. One movement emphasises the authority of reason, and the other, the authority of the Church, in things religious. Later, there is another liberal movement represented by such men as Frederic Denison Maurice and F. W. Robertson, — a departure from the rigidity of traditional theology, with the usual controversy and persecution which such movements call forth.

Again, we meet with the celebrated "Essays and Reviews" controversy. On the liberal side, we have a number of papers, independently prepared by different writers, containing many views in harmony with the spirit and results of the "Higher Criticism." The weakness of the dogmas of inspiration and inerrancy of the Scriptures is pointed out. The traditional views of miracles are opposed, and the irreconcilableness of the Mosaic cosmogony with the views of modern science is affirmed. This series of "Essays" provoked controversy; and there is a rejoinder in the form of another series, likewise independently written, representing more conservative positions. Still later, we find the methods and results of the "Higher Criticism" gaining ground, and traditional theology retreating gradually under the tremendous pressure of a more liberal and more enlightened thought.

Now, controversy, and especially religious and theological controversy, is usually apt to be fruitful of doubt. It very naturally raises the question in many minds as to the possibility of getting any stable and reliable basis for knowledge and faith; as to whether there be anything "final" in this domain; and whether, after all, Agnosticism be not the most rational, as well as the most reverent, attitude toward the fundamentals of religion. Such undoubtedly were the results in Tennyson's age. And the movement in the religious world during this period was very closely related to the tendencies in the scientific and philosophical worlds previously described. If science and philosophy throw doubt upon the so-called "Eternal Verities" with which the Christian religion is especially concerned, some might say, we can still fall back upon the authority of the Church and Holy Scripture. But with the infallible authority of these impeached by the results of reverent Christian scholarship itself, what course is left to the troubled and inquiring mind? Agnosticism was the reply which many serious-minded men gave to the question.

Now, Tennyson was profoundly in touch with his age. There were not many men who understood it better than he. He had his finger on its pulse, and his ear upon its breast; so that he heard its very heart-beat. He was acquainted with its problems, and he knew also the tremendous issues involved in the attitude of his age toward them. On the side of being, a crass Materialism cancels the reality of a personal God, a self-determining spirit, and an immortal soul. On the side of knowledge, a helpless Agnosticism excludes us from their presence. It tells us we have erected our altars to an Unknown God, whom, or which, we have been ignorantly worshipping. It affirms, also, constitutional impotency of man in dealing with his reality and immortality as a personal spirit. Tennyson had an almost morbid appreciation of the vital significance of belief in these supposed realities for human life; and, seeing this belief powerfully assailed, he addressed himself earnestly to their consideration. *Earnestly*, let it be said, for there are few poets who have realised the ethical obligations of their art more than Tennyson did. With him the end of art was not art itself. "Art for Art's sake" was a maxim which he openly rejected. Art must subserve an ethical end. It must be a vehicle for the good.

"Art for Art's sake! Hail, truest Lord of Hell!
  Hail Genius, Master of the Moral Will!
'The filthiest of all paintings painted well
  Is mightier than the purest painted ill!'
Yes, mightier than the purest painted well,
  So prone are we toward the broad way to Hell."

Thus he characterised "Art for Art's sake" "instead of Art for Art — and — Man's sake."[1] His son says: "These lines in a measure expressed his strong and sorrowful conviction, that the English were beginning to forget what was, in Voltaire's words, the glory of English literature — 'No nation has treated in poetry moral ideas with more energy and depth than the English nation.'"[2] He adds further, that his father quoted George Sand's words: "L'art pour art est un vain mot: l'art pour le vrai, l'art pour le

[1] Memoir, vol. ii., p. 92.   [2] Ibid.

beau et le bon, voilà la religion que je cherche."[1]   The "calling" of the poet, in Tennyson's view, is a responsible one, and he must be obedient to it.   This seems to be the lesson of *Merlin and the Gleam*, which the author himself professed to exemplify.   In short, Tennyson felt that the poet must not work "without a conscience or an aim," and his aim must be primarily an ethical one.   It is his business, through his art, to help men live this life as it ought to be lived.   Life, however, cannot thus be lived if we rob it of great hopes, beliefs, and ideals.   The poet must proclaim and maintain these if it be possible.   The most important of them refer to God, freedom, and the soul's destiny.   These give meaning and worth to life.   These are "the mighty hopes which make us men."   But the age assails them, denies them, giving strong reasons for its unfaith.   The effect of this upon human life must be discouraging and

1 Memoir, vol. ii., p. 92, note.

demoralising. A Godless world — with
"dust and ashes all that is!" What inspiration then; what motive power can
be brought to bear upon man to live his
life — to enable him to suffer, to endure,
to love, to battle for the True and Just?
If we "live and move and have our being"
in Matter and Law, instead of in "God
the Father;" if, in the essential elements
of our nature, we are merely "cunning
casts in clay," instead of self-determining
spiritual agents — responsible for conduct;
if the grave be the goal of man's endeavor,
and there be no "life everlasting;" then
the beliefs and ideals which condition
human life and progress lose their inspiring and impelling force.

This was the situation as Tennyson saw
it in the light of the tendencies of the age.
It stirred the great deeps of his soul, and
aroused him to most earnest consideration
of "the reasons for the faith" which much
of the science and philosophy of the time
denied, hoping, in consequence, to be

able, by means of his art, to give some helpful message to his fellow-men. And this earnest consideration was an *honest* consideration, also. Tennyson was conservative by nature, and more or less predisposed to favor the Theistic and Christian beliefs in which he had been nurtured, and the significance of which he so thoroughly appreciated and emphasised. But, on the other hand, he could not rest in a blind dogmatism. He loved the truth, and was desirous of knowing it and of maintaining it. The Welsh motto, "The truth against the world," which he sent to the Tennyson Society of Philadelphia,[1] illustrates the character of the man. He would not close his eyes to the truth if it made against his cherished predispositions or beliefs. Blind authority could never furnish a permanent refuge for him. An unreasoned or an unreasonable faith could not satisfy him. What he wrote of Hallam, was true of himself:

[1] Memoir, vol. ii., p. 91.

" He would not make his judgment blind,
He faced the spectres of the mind."

How true these words are in their appli-
cation to him will be manifest as we
carefully follow him in his consideration of the great questions of God, Freedom, and Immortality.

GOD

"Thou canst not prove the Nameless."

. . . . . .

"For nothing worthy proving can be proven,
    Nor yet disproven: wherefore thou be wise,
    Cleave ever to the sunnier side of doubt,
    And cling to Faith."

The Ancient Sage.

THE problem of knowledge is the most conspicuous problem of Modern Philosophy. Not knowledge of the various objects of the particular sciences, but *knowledge as knowledge*, — knowledge in its origin, nature, reality, and extent, — these are the questions which have pre-eminently engaged the speculative mind from Descartes to Herbert Spencer. In working out a solution of the problem, some have been led to the conclusion, that the mind as knowing mind — the mind as "Reason," or "Understanding," or "Intellect" — is incompetent to attain unto reality. Hence knowledge is not real; or, it is knowledge merely of the phenomenal — of reality as it appears, and not of reality as it is in itself. But the mind, they further affirm, is more than "Reason," "Understanding," or "Intellect." It is "Practical Reason," "Intuitive Reason," "Faith," or "Believing Soul," and as such, it is able to attain unto that reality from which "Pure Reason" excludes her. However wide their differences in detail, this is the general position of such writers as Kant,[1] Jacobi,[2] Hamilton,[3] and Mansel.[4] This position, as it bears on the question under consid-

[1] Kritik der reinen Vernunft, 1781 ; 2d ed., revised, 1787. Eng. trans. by Max Müller, 2 vols., London, 1881. Also, Kritik der praktischen Vernunft, 1788. Eng. trans. by T. K. Abbot, 4th ed., London, 1889.

[2] Briefe über die Lehre Spinoza's, Berlin, 1785. 2d ed., enlarged, 1789. Also, David Hume über den Glauben, oder Idealismus und Realismus, Breslau, 1787.

[3] Lectures on Metaphysics, Edinburgh and London. 1865. Lectures xxxviii–xl.

[4] The Limits of Religious Thought Examined, 1858. Also article, "Metaphysics," Encyclopædia Britannica, 8th ed.

eration, means, that God is unknowable
to the "Reason" or "Understanding"
of man; but is nevertheless apprehensible through the "Practical Reason" or
through "Faith." Tennyson takes essentially the same position.[1] That is, our
poet regards God in his essential being
and nature as unknowable. He is not an
object of proof or knowledge, but rather
an object of faith. He makes a distinction between the knowing mind and believing mind. The Agnostic is right
when he says God is the unprovable — the
unknowable. But he is wrong when he
affirms that, therefore, the human mind is
shut out from God — that He is an unat-
tainable Reality to the mind of man.
Faith transcends reason, and lays hold
upon God. Knowledge deals with the
phenomenal, but faith deals with the
noumenal. There are two poems in which
this position is especially revealed, and

[1] So do his contemporaries, Carlyle, in *Sartor
Resartus;* and Browning, in *La Saisiaz, Ferishtah's
Fancies, Francis Furini,* etc.

these poems are peculiarly personal.
They are *In Memoriam*, and *The Ancient
Sage*. In the prologue to *In Memoriam*,
which was written practically after the
rest of the poem was completed, and
which, in a sense, seems to sum up his
belief after many years of struggle with
doubt, he says: there is a domain of
knowledge and a domain of faith. These
are not contradictory. The domain of
faith merely lies beyond the reach of
knowledge. Knowledge "is of things
we see." It is capable of growth, —

"A beam in darkness, let it grow."

But it is always limited to "things we
see." Of course he means by "seeing"
here, not merely sense-perception, but
also the "seeing" of the reason — what
we ordinarily call proof. Knowledge is
confined to what can be known through
the senses, and to what can be rationally
inferred or demonstrated. But beyond
the limits of sense and reason there lies

the great world of reality, which can be entered alone by faith. This distinction is manifest in the very first verse of the prologue : —

> "Strong Son of God, immortal Love,
>   Whom we, that have not seen thy face,
>   By faith, and faith alone, embrace,
> Believing where we cannot prove."

Here, in the poet's judgment, is a great reality — God revealed in Christ — which is a reality to be grasped by faith alone. It is unprovable, so we must believe "where we cannot prove." Later in the prologue, addressing this same reality, God in Christ, he says : —

> " We have but faith : we cannot know ;
>   For knowledge is of things we see ;
>   And yet we trust it comes from thee,
> A beam in darkness : let it grow."

As we shall see later, this distinction which he makes between faith and knowledge, and which he applies here to the mind's relation to God as revealed in Christ, is an indication of his views in other portions of *In Memoriam*, concerning the mind's capacity to know God in His metaphysical nature.

When we turn to *The Ancient Sage*, which is one of the most philosophical of his poems, we find this position presented in quite an elaborate form. This poem is pronounced by Miss Weld, Tennyson's niece, to be even more subjective than *In Memoriam*.[1] And Tennyson himself wrote concerning it: "The whole poem is very personal. The passages about 'Faith' and the 'Passion of the Past' were more especially my own personal feelings."[2] The poem represents a youth "worn from wasteful living," in conversation with an ancient sage. The youth has in his hand "a scroll of verse." The sage asks the privilege of reading it. It contains agnostic and materialistic views of God, life, and immortality. With reference to God it says: —

[1] Contemporary Review, 1893.
[2] Memoir, vol. ii., p. 319.

" How far thro' all the bloom and brake
    That nightingale is heard !
What power but the bird's could make
    This music in the bird ?
How summer-bright are yonder skies,
    And earth as fair in hue !
And yet what sign of aught that lies
    Behind the green and blue ?
But man to-day is fancy's fool
    As man hath ever been.
The nameless Power, or Powers, that rule
    Were never heard or seen."

Here we have a thorough-going Agnosticism, and, indeed, one of its lowest forms,
which limits all knowledge to what the
senses reveal.   It hears the "music in the
bird," but can recognise no other Power as
the author of it than the power of the bird
itself.   It sees the summer-brightness of
the skies, and the fair hue of the earth, but
to it the heavens declare not the glory
of God, nor does the firmament show His
handiwork.   Its language is merely —

" How summer-bright are yonder skies,
    And earth as fair in hue !
And yet what sign of aught that lies
    Behind the green and blue ? "

Man is, and ever has been, "fancy's fool"
with reference to that which lies beyond
the domain of sense; and, so far as sense
is concerned, —

> " The nameless Power, or Powers, that rule
> Were never heard or seen."

Now Tennyson, through the reply of the
sage, rebukes this kind of Agnosticism.
He calls attention to man's inner being,
with its power of discernment, as distinguished from the outer being of sense,
and says : —

> " If thou would'st hear the Nameless, and wilt dive
> Into the Temple-cave of thine own self,
> There, brooding by the central altar, thou
> May'st haply learn the Nameless hath a voice,
> By which thou wilt abide, if thou be wise,
> As if thou knewest, tho' thou canst not know ;
> For Knowledge is the swallow on the lake
> That sees and stirs the surface-shadow there
> But never yet hath dipt into the abysm,
> The Abysm of all Abysms, beneath, within
> The blue of sky and sea, the green of earth,
> And in the million-millionth of a grain
> Which cleft and cleft again for evermore,
> And ever vanishing, never vanishes,

To me, my son, more mystic than myself,
Or even than the Nameless is to me.
   And when thou sendest thy free soul thro
      heaven,
Nor understandest bound nor boundlessness,
Thou seest the Nameless of the hundred names.
   And if the Nameless should withdraw from all
Thy frailty counts most real, all thy world
Might vanish like thy shadow in the dark."

Here we see that it is not by sense, but by diving " into the Temple-cave " of one's own being, that the Nameless, or God, is to be apprehended. There we learn that the Nameless has a voice. Nor, looking at the outer world, is it by knowledge that God is to be found, —

   " For Knowledge is the swallow on the lake "

merely skimming along the surface; never dipping into the abysm. Dip into the abysm, and, in your failure to understand its bounds or boundlessness, it is then that your soul sees God.

But the sage continues to read the "scroll of verse," which persists in unfolding its agnostic positions.

" And since — from when this earth began —
　The Nameless never came
Among us, never spake with man,
　And never named the Name " —

Here the sage stops to make a reply,
in which he calls attention to the limits
of the demonstrating or proving mind, and
to the province of faith.

"Thou canst not prove the Nameless, O my son,
　Nor canst thou prove the world thou movest in,
Thou canst not prove that thou art body alone,
Nor canst thou prove that thou art spirit alone,
Nor canst thou prove that thou art both in one :
Thou canst not prove thou art immortal, no
Nor yet that thou art mortal — nay my son,
Thou canst not prove that I, who speak with
　thee,
Am not thyself in converse with thyself,
For nothing worthy proving can be proven,
Nor yet disproven."

Here the limits of rational proof are
pointed out: there are a great many
things, some of which we regard as most
real and true, which neither admit of proof
nor disproof.　They do not lie within the
domain of knowledge, — of that which is

capable of rational proof or demonstration,
— nor, indeed, within the domain of disproof. They belong not to the field of
sense or reason. God is one of these
realities. What then? Complete Agnosticism? No! Man is more than sense
and reason. He is believing soul. He
has the power of faith. "Wherefore,"
says the sage, —

> "thou be wise,"

since —

> "nothing worthy proving can be proven,
> Nor yet disproven:
>
> Cleave ever to the sunnier side of doubt,
> And cling to Faith beyond the forms of Faith!
> She reels not in the storm of warring words,
> She brightens at the clash of 'Yes' and 'No,'
> She sees the Best that glimmers thro' the Worst,
> She feels the Sun is hid but for a night,
> She spies the summer thro' the winter bud,
> She tastes the fruit before the blossom falls,
> She hears the lark within the songless egg,
> She finds the fountain where they wail'd
> 'Mirage'!"

The lesson is taught here that there is
a power of mind which sees what sense

and reason cannot see. And, so far as
it concerns the question under consideration, we are told that —

" Thou canst not prove the Nameless,"

but we are not, therefore, to doubt his
reality, but rather to "cling to Faith."
She penetrates through the veil of sense
and reason; she sees the reality from
which they are shut out.

But, turning again to the "scroll of
verse," it continues with reference to
God : —

" What Power ? aught akin to Mind,
    The mind in me and you ?
  Or power as of the Gods gone blind
    Who see not what they do ? "

That is, it is asked whether this Power
behind the veil of sense is a mind like
ourselves, or, noting the imperfection of
the world, whether it is merely a blind,
unconscious, or, it may be, irrational,
blundering power.

The sage replies, that there are some

who, despite the defects, can only account
for "this house of ours" by attributing
its workmanship to the Gods.   But in
this answer the poet again tells us that
God is not known, but only felt.

"But some in yonder city hold, my son,
   That none but Gods could build this house of
      ours,
   So beautiful, vast, various, so beyond
   All work of man, yet, like all work of man,
   A beauty with defect —— till That which knows,
   And is not known, but felt thro' what we feel
   Within ourselves is highest, shall descend
   On this half-deed, and shape it at the last
   According to the Highest in the Highest."

But the Agnosticism in the scroll continues.   It affirms Time to be the only
Power and Ruler in the world.

"What Power but the Years that make
      And break the vase of clay,
   And stir the sleeping earth, and wake
      The bloom that fades away?
   What rulers but the Days and Hours
      That cancel weal with woe,
   And wind the front of youth with flowers,
      And cap our age with snow?"

But the sage again calls attention to the limits or superficiality of knowledge. Time is merely a conditioning form of knowledge. It is relative — subjective. It does not apply to reality. The mind, hampered by this form of Time, can, therefore, only know a phenomenal world. The unfortunate results of our mental impotency — of knowledge as conditioned by the Time-form — are seen in our views of Deity, to whom the Time-category is not applicable.

" The days and hours are ever glancing by,
And seem to flicker past thro' sun and shade,
Or short, or long, as Pleasure leads, or Pain ;
But with the Nameless is nor Day nor
        Hour;
Tho' we, thin minds, who creep from thought to
        thought,
Break into ' Thens' and ' Whens' the Eternal
        Now :
This double seeming of the single world ! —
My words are like the babblings in a dream
Of nightmare, when the babblings break the
        dream.
But thou be wise in this dream-world of ours,

Nor take thy dial for thy deity,
But make the passing shadow serve thy will." [1]

We see thus that in these two great poems, *In Memoriam,* and *The Ancient*

[1] This subjectivity and relativity of Time, with its inapplicability to the Deity, is a positive position with Tennyson. Several times, before writing *The Ancient Sage*, he calls our attention to it in his poetry. In *The Princess*, he says : —

> " To your question now,
> Which touches on the workman and his work.
> Let there be light and there was light: 'tis so :
> For was, and is, and will be, are but is ;
> And all creation is one act at once,
> The birth of light : but we that are not all,
> As parts, can see but parts, now this, now that,
> And live, perforce, from thought to thought, and make
> One act a phantom of succession : thus
> Our weakness somehow shapes the shadow, Time."

The poet takes the same position in regard to the subjective or relative nature of Time in *De Profundis;* denying its applicability to God. The spirit of the newly born child is spoken of as follows : —

> " O dear Spirit half-lost
> In thine own shadow and this fleshly sign
> That thou art thou — who wailest being born
> And banish'd into mystery, and the pain
> Of this divisible-indivisible world
> Among the numerable-innumerable
> Sun, sun, and sun, thro' finite-infinite space
> In finite-infinite Time — our mortal veil
> And shatter'd phantom of that infinite One," etc.

Sage, Tennyson draws a distinction between knowledge, which deals with the
phenomenal, and faith, which deals with
the *noumenal*. He affirms God, and, as
we shall see later, immortality, to be the
real world — not to be apprehended by
the knowing mind, but by the believing
soul. They belong, not to the province
of the knowable, but to the province of
the believable.

Now, this position was not dogmatically
or uncritically assumed by Tennyson.
He thought earnestly on this subject. It
is safe to say that he was familiar with
the so-called "proofs" of the being and
nature of God as they appear in Modern
Philosophy. For, of the writers with
whose works we have found him acquainted, Descartes, Locke, Berkeley, and
Kant have respectively discussed one or
more of them. Of these "proofs" or
arguments, the teleological or design
argument has always seemed the most
convincing. It points to the apparent

order and harmony, symmetry and proportion, adaptation of means to ends, in the
world, as evidences of design or purpose,
and infers from these the intelligence and
rationality of the World-Ground, or God.
Because of the prevalence of the mechanical conception of nature in Tennyson's
time, the design argument figured con-
spicuously in the scientific, philosophical,
and theological controversies of the age.
As a "proof" of the existence of an intel-
ligent Deity the argument had little force
with Tennyson. This is evident from
the following : —

> " That which we dare invoke to bless ;
>   Our dearest faith; our ghastliest doubt;
>   He, They, One, All ; within, without;
>   The Power in darkness whom we guess ;

> " I found Him not in world or sun,
>   Or eagle's wing, or insect's eye."

Here the poet confesses that he cannot
find God as Personal Intelligence in
Nature. The order and harmony of the
"worlds" and "suns" have usually been

regarded by teleologists as constituting
strong evidence in favor of their position.
But Tennyson says, —

"I found Him not in world or sun."

The wing of the bird has also been used
as a striking example of "final cause."
Huxley said that the difference between
the teleologist and mechanist is seen in
this: the former says that the bird has
wings in order that it may fly; whereas
the latter says that the bird flies because
it has wings.   But Tennyson says, he
finds Him not in "eagle's wing."   Furthermore, the eye has, with most theistic
writers, been regarded as a classic example of design or purpose in nature.   It
seems to reveal a remarkable adaptation
of means to end — of organ to function.
But despite this, Tennyson finds Him not
in "insect's eye."

Indeed, Tennyson does not find Nature
revealing design or purpose.   His poetry
reveals the fact that he appealed to

Nature more than once on this subject,
and always with the same result.   In the
fifty-fourth and fifty-fifth poems of *In
Memoriam*, where the question of a purpose in Nature is under consideration, he
confesses inadequacy of knowledge with
reference to a purpose of God in Nature,
and the necessity of faith in order to get
at Nature's "secret meaning."   In considering the final goal of ill (in the
form of pain and sin), and the tremendous
"profusion and waste" in Nature, he
says :—

> " Oh, yet we trust [not know] that somehow good
>   Will be the final goal of ill,
>   To pangs of nature, sins of will,
> Defects of doubt, and taints of blood ;
>
> " That nothing walks with aimless feet ;
>   That not one life shall be destroy'd,
>   Or cast as rubbish to the void,
> When God hath made the pile complete ;
>
> " That not a worm is cloven in vain ;
>   That not a moth with vain desire
>   Is shrivell'd in a fruitless fire,
> Or but subserves another's gain."

But in regard to all this we have no knowledge, but only trust.　For he adds:—

> " Behold, we know not anything ;
> I can but trust that good shall fall
> At last — far off — at last, to all,
> And every winter change to spring."

And then follow those most pathetic
words:—

> " So runs my dream: but what am I?
> An infant crying in the night:
> An infant crying for the light:
> And with no language but a cry."

And, again, in the fifty-fifth poem,
where he is considering the question of
immortality from the standpoint of God's
purpose in Nature.　He does not find
Nature revealing a purpose of God; or, if
anything, revealing hostility to His purpose as manifest in the soul of man.

> " The wish, that of the living whole
> No life may fail beyond the grave,
> Derives it not from what we have
> The likest God within the soul?

" Are God and Nature then at strife,
      That Nature lends such evil dreams ?
      So careful of the type she seems,
   So careless of the single life ;

" That I, considering everywhere
      Her secret meaning in her deeds,
      And finding that of fifty seeds
   She often brings but one to bear,

" I falter where I firmly trod,
      And falling with my weight of cares
      Upon the great world's altar-stairs
   That slope through darkness up to God,

" I stretch lame hands of faith, and grope,
      And gather dust and chaff, and call
      To what I feel is Lord of all,
   And faintly trust the larger hope."

But he seems also to be suspicious of
the other theistic arguments, if we rightly
interpret him.   These "prove" the existence of a Perfect Being from the necessary idea of such a being which we possess ;
and, secondly, the existence of an eternal
First Cause from the existence of a finite,
changing, dependent world.   In regard to
these arguments Tennyson says : —

> " I found Him not in world or sun,
>   Or eagle's wing, or insect's eye ;
>   *Nor thro' the questions men may try,*
>   *The petty cobwebs we have spun.*"

It seems quite probable that Tennyson here, in the words "the questions men may try," refers to the other philosophical arguments for the existence of God. They occur in immediate connection with the words in which he rejects the design argument. They fail to reveal God to him. As "proofs" they carry no force of conviction. So utterly do they fall short of their purpose that the poet speaks of them almost contemptuously. He pronounces them to be nothing more than —

> " The petty cobwebs we have spun."

This rejection of the traditional "proofs" of the being and nature of God is in harmony with his general position already stated. It means —

> " Thou canst not prove the Nameless."

It means, God is —

> " That which knows,
> And is not known."

It means, concerning God, —

> "We have but faith : we cannot know."

It means, God is, so far as sense and reason are concerned, —

> " The Power in darkness whom we guess."

But, on the other hand, these very poems which reveal the impotency of the mind so far as its capacity to know God is concerned, also point out the necessity of falling back upon another power of man — faith.   If an "intelligible First Cause " be not "deducible from physical phenomena," as Tennyson affirmed, in his vote on this question when under consideration in the society of "Apostles," in Cambridge;[1] if He be not revealed "in world or sun," or "eagle's wing," or "insect's eye;" if He be not disclosed to us " in the questions men may try," He *is* revealed to man through faith.   The In-

[1] Memoir, vol. i., p. 44, note.

visible to the eye of sense becomes
visible to the eye of faith. The unprovable and unknowable to the demonstrating reason becomes the apprehensible to
the believing soul. Wherefore, we are
enjoined to —

" Cling to Faith beyond the forms of Faith."

We can believe "where we cannot prove."

And what kind of God does faith
reveal? According to Tennyson, faith
reveals a *personal* God. This is evident
when we glance at the following poems.[1]
Take, for example, his little poem entitled
The Human Cry : —

I.

" Hallowed be Thy name — Halleluiah !
    Infinite Ideality !
    Immeasurable Reality !
    Infinite Personality !
Hallowed be Thy name — Halleluiah !"

[1] The distinction between Christian faith and philosophical faith is not very marked in Tennyson. In
some of these poems he undoubtedly refers to Christian faith. In *In Memoriam*, he refers now to one, then
to the other. In *The Ancient Sage*, he apparently refers to philosophical faith. However, with him, their
essential content is the same.

II.

" We feel we are nothing, — for all is Thou and in
        Thee ;
    We feel we are something, — *that* also has come
        from Thee ;
    We know we are nothing, — but Thou wilt help
        us to be.
    Hallowed be Thy name — Halleluiah ! "

Again, the entire prologue to *In Memoriam* declares God as personal being to be
revealed to us by faith.   Indeed, it recognises God as revealed in the person of
Christ : —

" Strong Son of God, immortal Love,
        Whom we, that have not seen thy face,
        By faith, and faith alone, embrace,
    Believing where we cannot prove ;

" Thine are these orbs of light and shade ;
        Thou madest Life in man and brute ;
        Thou madest Death ; and lo, thy foot
    Is on the skull which thou hast made.

" Thou wilt not leave us in the dust :
        Thou madest man, he knows not why,
        He thinks he was not made to die ;
    And thou hast made him : thou art just.

" Thou seemest human and divine,
 The highest, holiest manhood, thou :
 Our wills are ours, we know not how ;
Our wills are ours, to make them thine.

" Our little systems have their day ;
 They have their day and cease to be :
 They are but broken lights of thee,
And thou, O Lord, art more than they.

" We have but faith : we cannot know ;
 For knowledge is of things we see ;
 And yet we trust it comes from thee,
A beam in darkness : let it grow.

" Let knowledge grow from more to more,
 But more of reverence in us dwell ;
 That mind and soul, according well,
May make one music as before,

" But vaster. We are fools and slight ;
 We mock thee when we do not fear :
 But help thy foolish ones to bear ;
Help thy vain worlds to bear thy light.

" Forgive what seem'd my sin in me ;
 What seem'd my worth since I began ;
 For merit lives from man to man,
And not from man, O Lord, to thee.

" Forgive my grief for one removed,
 Thy creature, whom I found so fair.
 I trust he lives in thee, and there
I find him worthier to be loved.

" Forgive these wild and wandering cries,
    Confusions of a wasted youth ;
      Forgive them where they fail in truth,
And in thy wisdom make me wise."

This is a prayer. The very prayer itself involves the recognition of a personal God revealed in Christ. Every verse of the prayer, except one, distinctly specifies as personal the nature of the Being addressed. And the opening verse tells us He is embraced alone by faith. And so in the poems entitled *Doubt and Prayer*, *Faith*, and *God and the Universe*, faith apprehends God as personal being. So far, then, as the being and nature of God are concerned, according to Tennyson, they are not matters of proof or knowledge, but of faith.

Now, when we try to further determine the nature of God as *Love*, we find our poet holding the same position. God's nature as Love is not a matter of knowledge, but of faith. He struggled with this question also in the light of what

science and philosophy had to say. He
was greatly interested in the theory of
organic evolution, and in the Darwinian
explanation of it. This "struggle for
existence," with its dreadful suffering, is
an awful fact. Nature, in her onward
course, has left a trail of blood reaching
far back into the ages. Tennyson was
profoundly impressed by this fact. He
made his appeal to Nature to find out
whether the great Author of Nature is
essential Love. Such an appeal seemed
to indicate that He is not. There is a
very significant statement by him on this
point recorded in the *Memoir*. He said,
with reference to the pain and imperfection of the world, which at times almost
impelled him to doubt the intelligence
and love of God: "Yet God *is* love, tran-
scendent, all-pervading! We do not get
this faith from Nature or the world. If
we look at Nature alone, full of perfection and imperfection, she tells us that
God is disease, murder, and rapine. We

get this faith from ourselves, from what is highest within us, which recognises that there is not one fruitless pang, just as there is not one lost good." [1]   This faith is the trust he attributes to man in the words quoted above, and which he speaks of in the fifty-fourth poem of *In Memoriam* : —

> " Oh yet we trust that somehow good
>   Will be the final goal of ill,
>   To pangs of nature," etc.

This appeal to Nature was, of course, from the standpoint of sense and reason. In Tennyson's case it was often made through science, for, as previously stated, he was a careful student of science.   But his appeal results in no proof of God's love.   This attribute of God's nature must also be apprehended by faith.   Faith alone can discern God as Love in the midst of the physical suffering of the world.   So we are enjoined, in his little poem entitled *Faith*, to —

[1] Memoir, vol. i., p. 314.

" Doubt no longer that the Highest is the wisest
and the best,
Let not all that saddens Nature blight thy hope
or break thy rest,
Quail not at the fiery mountain, at the ship-
wreck, or the rolling
Thunder, or the rending earthquake, or the
famine, or the pest!"

But he not only considered this problem
of the love of God from the standpoint of
suffering, as manifest in the physical
world, but also from the standpoint of its
broader aspects, as treated by philosophy.
He took into consideration the mental
suffering of the world, — the suffering
caused by sin; yea, the sin itself. Not
only the "pangs of nature" and "taints
of blood," but also the "defects of
doubt," "the sins of will," etc., were
considered in their bearing upon the
nature and character of God as Love.
And here he came to the same conclusion:
that, so far as knowledge is concerned,
we cannot find God as Love in the mental
and moral evil of the world. We can

only find him as such through hope, trust, and faith. *In Memoriam*, taken as a whole, evidences this position. As Tennyson himself said concerning this great poem: "The different moods of sorrow as in a drama are dramatically given, and my conviction that fear, doubts, and suffering will find answer and relief only through Faith in a God of Love." [1]

This, too, is hinted in *The Ancient Sage*. The "scroll of verse," to which reference has been made, continues to point to evidence that Time is the great Power and Ruler of the world, and presents a melancholy description of His fearful ravages. To this the sage replies:—

"My son, the world is dark with grief and graves,
So dark that men cry out against the heavens."

But from what follows, it seems the sage means to intimate that this is merely the world as it appears to sense and reason. Faith, however, presents a different picture:—

[1] Memoir, vol. i., pp. 304, 305.

" Who knows but that the darkness is in man ?
  The doors of Night may be the gates of Light ;
  For wert thou born or blind or deaf, and then
  Suddenly heal'd, how would'st thou glory in all
  The splendours and the voices of the world !
  And we, the poor earth's dying race, and yet
  No phantoms, watching from a phantom shore,
  Await the last and largest sense to make
  The phantom walls of this illusion fade,
  And show us that the world is wholly fair."

And again, in one of his later poems, entitled *Doubt and Prayer*, the fact is pointed out, that through sin we are led to misinterpret the sorrowful experiences of life, which are God's providences, attributing them to " Blind Fate." And the poet prays that he may learn the lesson of faith on this point, which is, that Love, not " Blind Fate," rules the world.

" Tho' Sin, too oft, when smitten by Thy rod,
  Rail at ' Blind Fate ' with many a vain ' Alas ! '
  From sin thro' sorrow into Thee we pass
  By that same path our true forefathers trod ;
  And let not Reason fail me, nor the sod
  Draw from my death Thy living flower and grass,
  Before I learn that Love, which is, and was
  My Father, and my Brother, and my God !

Steel me with patience ! soften me with grief !
Let blow the trumpet strongly while I pray,
Till this embattled wall of unbelief
My prison, not my fortress, fall away !
Then, if thou willest, let my day be brief,
So Thou wilt strike Thy glory thro' the day."

The Love of God, then, according to Tennyson's view, is rather a fact of faith than an object of knowledge. And this interpretation of his poetry is corroborated by external evidence. In a letter to Miss Emily Sellwood, afterward Lady Tennyson, he says : " 'Why has God created souls knowing they would sin and suffer ?' a question unanswerable. Man is greater than all animals because he is capable of moral good and evil, tho' perhaps dogs and elephants, and some of the higher mammalia have a little of this capability. God might have made me a beast ; but He thought good to give me power, to set Good and Evil before me, that I might shape my own path. The happiness, resulting from this power well exercised, must in the end exceed the mere physical

happiness of breathing, eating, and sleeping like an ox. Can we say that God pre-
fers higher happiness in some to a lower
happiness in all? It is a hard thing that
if I sin and fail I should be sacrificed to
the bliss of the Saints. Yet what reason-
able creature, if he could have been askt
beforehand, would not have said, 'Give
me the metaphysical power; let me be the
lord of my decisions; leave physical
quietude and dull pleasure to lower lives'?
All souls, methinks, would have answered
thus, and so had men suffered by their
own choice, as now by the necessity of
being born what they are, but there is no
answer to these questions except in a great
hope of universal good: and even then one
might ask, why has God made one to
suffer more than another, why is it not
meted equally to all? Let us be silent,
for we know nothing of these things, and
we trust there is One who knows all.
God cannot be cruel. If He were, the
heart could only find relief in the wildest

blasphemies, which would cease to be
blasphemies. God must be all powerful,
else the soul could never deem Him
worthy of her highest worship. Let us
leave it therefore to God, as to the wisest.
Who knows whether revelation be not
itself a veil to hide the glory of that
Love which we could not look upon
without marring our sight, and our onward
progress?"[1]

On the question, then, of the nature of
God as Love, we find Tennyson's teaching
to be, that it is not a matter of knowledge,
but of faith; and, however strong be the
evidence from Nature and human experience to the contrary, through faith we
may apprehend God as Love; through
faith we may be enabled —

> "To feel, altho' no tongue can prove,
>   That every cloud, that spreads above
>   And veileth love, itself is love."

Thus we have seen that Tennyson was
in sympathy with much of our modern

[1] Memoir, vol. i., pp. 170.

science and philosophy in their Agnosticism. God is, indeed, "the Unknown and
the Unknowable." But it is important
to note, that he did not rest in Agnosticism. He regarded it as merely half
the truth respecting God, and man's
capacity to reach Him. There is another
side to man's being. This, too, has its
legitimate domain — its field of realities.
This is faith. And, as he said to Locker-
Lampson, "Whatever is the object of
Faith cannot be the object of Reason. In
fine, Faith must be our guide." [1] If, as
perceiving mind and demonstrating reason, man is limited to the phenomenal; as
believing soul, he can transcend these
narrow bounds and pass from the "shadow"
to the substance; from the appearance to
the reality — to the Supreme Reality
"which Faith calls God, and Philosophy
calls the Absolute." Faith tells us that
God is; that He is Personal Intelligence,
and that He is Eternal Love. Thus

[1] Memoir, vol. ii., pp. 68, 69.

did our poet meet the Agnosticism of his age.

But Tennyson really reached a more speculative conclusion on this subject than is indicated above. He dealt not merely with the Agnostic, but also with the Materialist; and, in his ontological speculations, he came to conclusions with reference to the being and nature of God in perfect harmony with those of his Faith Philosophy. Let us take, for example, that speculative poem entitled *The Higher Pantheism*. This poem was sent by Tennyson to the Metaphysical Society, previously referred to, as undoubtedly expressive of his own personal views. It deals with the problems of ontology, — the ultimate nature of reality, and the relation of the finite to the Infinite. With reference to these problems we find him to be an Idealist. He declares all reality, in the final analysis, to be mentality. That is, there is only one kind of being, and that is Mind. He cancels the reality of the so-called corporeal or material world, — allowing it merely a phenomenal existence.   An examination of the poem makes this evident at once : —

" The sun, the moon, the stars, the seas, the hills
  and the plains —
 Are not these, O Soul, the Vision of Him who
  reigns ?

" Is not the Vision He ? tho' He be not that which
  He seems ?
 Dreams are true while they last, and do we not
  live in dreams?

" Earth, these solid stars, this weight of body and
  limb,
 Are they not sign and symbol of thy division from
  Him ?

" Dark is the world to thee : thyself art the reason
  why ;
 For is He not all but that which has power to feel
  ' I am I ' ?

" Glory about thee, without thee ; and thou fulfillest
  thy doom,
 Making Him broken gleams, and a stifled splen-
  dour and gloom.

" Speak to Him thou for He hears, and Spirit with
  Spirit can meet —
 Closer is He than breathing, and nearer than
  hands and feet.

5

" God is law, say the wise ; O Soul, and let us
     rejoice,
   For if He thunder by law the thunder is yet His
     voice.

" Law is God, say some; no God at all, says the
     fool ;
   For all we have power to see is a straight staff
     bent in a pool ;

" And the ear of man cannot hear, and the eye of
     man cannot see ;
" But if we could see and hear, this Vision — were
     it not He ? "

The most thorough-going Idealism is
revealed in this poem. The reality of
corporeal or material objects is annihi-
lated, and minds only are affirmed to exist,
— the Infinite Mind and finite minds.

" For is He not all but that which has power to
     feel ' I am I ' ? "

That is, God, who is personal (he uses
the personal pronoun), is all but self-
conscious finite being, — that finite being
which has the power to feel " I am I."
Corporeal beings have no such power of
self-consciousness, hence they have no

reality. Only self-conscious being really
is. All else is merely phenomenal.
This is, of course, Idealism.

But the form of Idealism, whether subjective or objective, revealed in this poem,
is not so easily determined. Subjective
Idealism declares corporeal things to have
no other reality than as "ideas" in the
mind. As Berkeley affirmed, their being
consists in their being perceived. "Their
esse is *percipi.*" [1] Cancel mind, and there
is no matter. Objective Idealism, on the
other hand, affirms, that so-called corporeal
objects have something more than mere
subjective existence — existence merely
as "ideas" in the perceiving mind. They
have an *objective* or *extra-mental* existence;
but not in the form of independent, material things, as assumed and conceived of
by uncritical thought; but rather as defi-
nite modes or forms of activity or energis-
ing of the Infinite Mind. Of these two

[1] Of the Principles of Human Knowledge, pt. i.
sec. 3.

kinds of Idealism, Tennyson leans toward
the latter.   In the first couplet of the
above poem, such supposed substantial
realities as the sun, the moon, the stars,
the seas, etc., are represented to us as
having only the being of a "vision" —
they are the soul's "vision" of God.
Now the word *vision* can either refer to
the mental act of perception, or to the
object perceived.   In both instances we
might have subjective Idealism, because
the object perceived might be merely a
mental one.   But the second couplet of
the poem helps us in our interpretation.
Here he evidently uses the word "vision"
in the sense of the object perceived, and
indicates it to be an extra-mental object.
He identifies the "vision" with God
himself.

"Is not the Vision He? tho' He be not that
    which He seems?"

And again, in the fourth couplet, he
says:—

"Dark is the world to thee: thyself art the reason
    why;
For is He not all but that which has the power
    to feel ' I am I '? "

And again, in the last couplet: —

" And the ear of man cannot hear, and the eye of
    man cannot see;
But if we could see and hear, this Vision — were
    it not He ? "

But, furthermore, we have not only
Idealism, and probably objective Idealism,
here; but also Theistic Idealism. And
this is important, as bearing on the question under consideration, namely, Tennyson's view of the nature of God. There
is an Idealism which is Pantheism. It
holds the position, that all being is one
and psychic in its nature, — but *not personal*. It cancels both the personality of
God and of man — making man merely a
mode or manifestation of the Infinite.
But not so with Tennyson. His " Higher
Pantheism " is not Pantheism. It is
Idealistic Theism. He distinctly affirms

all being to be personal spirit. And there are two kinds of personal spirit: God, the infinite Spirit, and all finite beings which have the power of self-consciousness; "the power to feel 'I am I.'" Every couplet of this poem, save one, uses the personal pronoun in speaking of God. And the third and fourth couplets especially declare the distinct individuality and personality of the finite spirit.

We have, then, in this speculative poem, both a declaration against Materialism and against Pantheism. Matter has no reality. If it exist at all, it has only phenomenal existence. Mind, or self-conscious being, is the only true reality. And there are two kinds of minds or personal spirits, — the Infinite and the finite; and their intimate relation is declared in those beautiful words: —

" Speak to Him thou for He hears, and Spirit
      with Spirit can meet —
   Closer is He than breathing, and nearer than
      hands and feet."

Now, if we turn to other poems, we find
this idealistic view of the ultimate nature
of reality at least indirectly confirmed by
his repeated affirmation that the so-called
material world has merely a phenomenal
existence. He pronounces it a "phantom" and a "shadow." In *De Profundis*,
the true world is not the one we see. We
see merely a "shadow-world." The child
is represented as coming —

"out of the deep,
From that true world within the world we see,
Whereof our world is but the bounding shore — "

Man is represented here as having —

"drawn to this shore lit by the suns and moons
And all the shadows."

In *The Ancient Sage*, there are several
references to this "phantom-shore," or
"shadow-world." He preserves our *reality*
as spirits, but affirms the *phantom nature*
of the world. He says : —

"And we, the poor earth's dying race, and yet
No phantoms, watching from a phantom shore."

Again, in describing a trance experience, to which he was subject, he speaks of the nature of this experience as one of "utter clearness."

> " and thro' loss of Self
> The gain of such large life as match'd with ours
> Were Sun to spark — unshadowable in words,
> Themselves but shadows of a shadow-world."

Again, in the poem entitled *God and the Universe*, he refers to "the myriad world" as God's "shadow": —

> " Spirit, nearing yon dark portal at the limit of thy
>   human state,
>   Fear not thou the hidden purpose of that Power
>   which alone is great,
>   Nor the myriad world, His shadow, nor the
>   Silent Opener of the Gate."

In all of these references, reality is denied to the corporeal world. It is merely a "phantom" — a "shadow" of God, the Spiritual.

This idealistic conception of reality is also brought out in a number of conversations of Tennyson which have been re-

corded. Mr. Frederick Locker-Lampson
informs us that, in a conversation he once
had with Tennyson, while gazing upon
the Alps, he said, "Perhaps this earth,
and all that is on it — storms, mountains,
cataracts, the sun and the skies — are the
Almighty: in fact, that such is our petty
nature, we cannot see Him, but we see
His shadow, as it were, a distorted
shadow."[1] Again, Mrs. Bradley has a
record in her diary of words uttered by
Tennyson in her presence, in January,
1869, as follows: "Yes, it is true that
there are moments when the flesh is
nothing to me, when I feel and know the
flesh to be the vision, God and the Spiritual the only real and true. Depend upon
it, the Spiritual *is* the real: it belongs to
one more than the hand and foot. You
may tell me that my hand and my foot
are only imaginary symbols of my existence, I could believe you; but you never,
never can convince me that the *I* is not an

[1] Memoir, vol. ii., p. 68.

eternal Reality, and that the Spiritual is not the true and real part of me."[1]   His son informs us, that in one of his "last talks" he said, "Spirit seems to me to be the reality of the world."[2]   Again, talking with Frederick Locker-Lampson "of the materialists," he said: "After all, what is matter?"   "I think it is merely the shadow of something greater than itself, and which we poor, shortsighted creatures cannot see."[3]

The only reality, then, in Tennyson's conception, is mind,—the Infinite and the finite.   God is, and He is personal.   Man is, and he is personal.   God and Man as personal being constitute the only reality, and between them exists a close relationship:—

"Speak to Him thou for He hears, and Spirit with Spirit can meet—
    Closer is He than breathing, and nearer than hands and feet."

[1] Memoir, vol. ii. p. 90.   [2] Ibid., p. 424.
                [3] Ibid., p. 69.

Thus we see, that Tennyson, in his more speculative thinking, came to essentially the same conclusions, with reference to the being and nature of God, as those attained in his Philosophy of Faith.

FREEDOM

Our wills are ours, we know not how;
Our wills are ours, to make them thine.

In Memoriam, Prologue, 4

. . . who wrought
Not Matter, nor the finite-infinite,
But this main-miracle, that thou art thou,
With power on thine own act and on the world.

De Profundis, II., ii.

ONE of the fundamental problems which has had, in nearly every age, a fascination for the speculative mind, is the problem of freedom, or free-will. From the time of Socrates down to the present, it has seriously engaged the philosophic world.[1] Its prominence in the scientific, philosophical, and theological thinking of Tennyson's age did not fail to arrest his attention, and, in

[1] See A. Alexander, Theories of the Will in the History of Philosophy, New York, 1898.

consequence, the question of freedom has received earnest consideration at his hands. However, his interest in this question, like his interest in the problems of God and immortality, was not merely speculative, but practical. He clearly saw, that this profound problem, however fascinating and engaging to the reflective mind, was not simply a problem of the philosopher's den, but one having a vital bearing on human life. And, indeed, he approached it from this point of view. We cannot give up "the mighty hopes that make us men," neither can we yield those fundamental beliefs which give life its supreme worth. The freedom of the will, in our poet's opinion, was one of these beliefs. On it rest the moral interests of life. But this is one of those great beliefs which the science and philosophy of the age threatened. The materialistic conception of man, which was so widely prevalent, was of course inconsistent with a belief in free agency. The sensationalistic psychology and philosophy, which regarded man as merely " a bundle of sensations," grouped according to mechanical laws, was also incompatible with such a belief, as Tennyson points out very forcibly in the *Promise of May*. The Transcendentalism of the age, as explained in the Introduction, put freedom into the category of the unknown and unknowable. Many of the most influential writers in Ethics, writing from the hedonistic or evolutional points of view, denied man's power of self-determination. In other words, here was one of the most vital beliefs of man assailed on all sides by some of the most dominant intellectual forces of the age. Tennyson was aware of this, and was conscious of its significance. He took the problem up, giving it serious consideration, and did not fail to put himself on record.

That he was deeply interested in this question of freedom, a careful examination of his poetry reveals. Such poems as those entitled *Will*, *Wages*, *In Memoriam*,

The Idylls of the King, De Profundis, Despair, The Ancient Sage, The Promise of May, By an Evolutionist, The Dawn, and *The Making of Man,* evidence this. Either explicitly, or by implication, they treat of the reality, mystery, responsibility, consequences, and goal of free-will.

Again, there is external evidence concerning Tennyson's interest in this question at our command, — evidence which shows also that his interest was not merely speculative, but practical, appreciating the important bearing of the question on human life. His son informs us, that " Free-will and its relation to the meaning of human life and to circumstance was latterly one of his most common subjects of conversation." [1] He records, also, his father as saying, "Take away the sense of individual responsibility and men sink into pessimism and madness." [2] Tennyson " wrote at the end of the poem 'Despair': 'In my boyhood I came across the Cal-

---

[1] Memoir, vol. i., p. 316. [2] Ibid., p. 317.

vinist Creed, and assuredly however unfathomable the mystery, if one cannot
believe in the freedom of the human will
as of the Divine, life is hardly worth
having.' " [1] His son further says, "The
lines that he oftenest repeated about Free-
will were,

' This main-miracle that thou art thou,
  With power on thine own act and on the world.'

Then he would enlarge upon man's con-
sequent moral obligations, upon the Law
which claims a free obedience, and upon
the pursuit of moral perfection (in imitation
of the Divine) to which man is called." [2]

Let us, then, inquire carefully into Tennyson's views on this important question.
And first, on the question of the *reality* of
free-will. An examination of his poetry
will disclose very clearly, indeed, that he
believed in its reality. If we turn to the
poem entitled *Will*, we find him recognising this endowment of man. His son says,

[1] Memoir, vol. i., p. 317.   [2] Ibid.

concerning the second part of this poem, in which the poet notes man's responsibility for the proper exercise of this endowment, and the ill consequences which follow an improper use of it, that it is "one of the last passages I heard him recite about Free-will."[1] The poem reads: —

I

"O well for him whose will is strong!
  He suffers, but he will not suffer long;
  He suffers, but he cannot suffer wrong:
  For him nor moves the loud world's random
     mock,
  Nor all Calamity's hugest waves confound,
  Who seems a promontory of rock,
  That, compass'd round with turbulent sound,
  In middle ocean meets the surging shock,
  Tempest-buffeted, citadel-crown'd.

II

"But ill for him who, bettering not with time,
  Corrupts the strength of heaven-descended Will,
  And ever weaker grows thro' acted crime,
  Or seeming-genial venial fault,
  Recurring and suggesting still!
  He seems as one whose footsteps halt,
  Toiling in immeasurable sand,
  And o'er a weary sultry land,

[1] Memoir, vol. i., p. 318.

> Far beneath a blazing vault,
> Sown in a wrinkle of the monstrous hill,
> The city sparkles like a grain of salt."

If we examine next the little poem entitled *Wages*, we find the reality of will — which means free-will — an implication of the poem. Here he contrasts the glory of warrior, orator, and song, with the glory of virtue — an achievement of will, or, more properly, will rightly exercised. The former are —

> " Paid with a voice flying by to be lost on an endless sea " —

but the glory of virtue is,

> "to fight, to struggle, to right the wrong."

Indeed, she really does not aim at glory at all. The only wages she asks are —

> "the glory of going on, and still to be."

Turning next to *In Memoriam*, we again find a recognition of the reality of freedom. In the prologue, there is an explicit declaration of man's freedom. We are told,—

> "Our wills are ours, we know not how ; "

and this declaration is repeated in explaining the object or purpose of this endowment, —

"Our wills are ours, to make them thine."

In poem LIV., in considering the purpose or goal of physical and moral evil, he again recognises the reality of will. Sin is here conceived of, not as mere animalism or bestiality, but as a wrong exercise of the will. In other words, he believes there are "sins of will."

Again, in poem LXXXV., he reveals to us his sense of responsibility, growing out of his consciousness of the possession of free agency.

"Yet none could better know than I,
    How much of act at human hands
    The sense of human will demands
By which we dare to live or die."

Again, in poem CXXXI., the reality of free-will receives recognition — as well as its immortality. It shall endure —

"When all that seems shall suffer shock."

Indeed, does not the poet in these words hint at a position which we have found to be characteristic of his teachings, namely, the difference between the psychical and the so-called corporeal or material? The latter is the *seeming* — that which seems — and therefore not the truly *real*. The "living will" belongs to the domain of the real — and it is destined to endure when the seeming, or phenomenal, "shall suffer shock." Tennyson's son informs us, that his father explained the words —

"O living will that shalt endure"

"as that which we know as Free-will, the higher and enduring part of man."[1] Furthermore, in this poem, the will is conceived of as the purifier of our deeds, and he enjoins it to —

"Rise in the spiritual rock,
Flow thro' our deeds and make them pure."

He also speaks here of a —

"faith that comes of self-control," —

[1] Memoir, vol. i., p. 319.

thus declaring again our self-determination, or free-will, to be a fact.

If we now turn our attention to *The Idylls of the King*, we meet with the same teaching. In those " spiritually central lines of the *Idylls* " it is manifest.

> " In moments when he feels he cannot die,
>   And knows himself no vision to himself,
>   Nor the high God a vision."

Here he affirms the reality of God and man, and also, of man's immortality. Before this, he has been speaking of moments when the material world, including even the human body, appears to belong merely to the world of seeming — the world of "vision" — the phenomenal world, and not to the world of reality. But man is a spirit — a person —

> " And knows himself no vision to himself,"

but rather as a reality, and a reality, too, which he feels cannot die. Now, Tennyson regards free-will, the "power over thine own act and on the world," as

of the very essence of personality. This
is evident from his poem, *De Profundis*,
which will be considered later. Hence, in
these "spiritually central lines of the
Idylls," we have a recognition of man's
power of self-determination.

Furthermore, is not free-will a fundamental implication of this entire series of
remarkable poems? The author, in the
words " To the Queen " appended to the
Idylls, says, that this " old imperfect tale,
new-old," shadows " Sense at war with
Soul." In other words, we have in these
poems the story of the conflict between
sense and spirit. " Arthur is intended to
be a man in whom the spirit has already
conquered and reigns supreme. It is
upon this that his kingship rests. His
task is to bring his realm into harmony
with himself, to build up a spiritual and
social order upon which his own character,
as the best and highest, shall be impressed.
In other words, he works for the uplifting
and purification of humanity. It is the

problem of civilization. His great enemies
in this task are not outward and visible, —
the heathen, — for these he overcomes and
expels. But the real foes that oppose
him to the end are the evil passions in the
hearts of men and women about him. So
long as these exist and dominate human
lives, the dream of a perfected society
must remain unrealized; and when they
get the upper hand, even its beginnings
will be destroyed. But the conflict is not
an airy, abstract strife; it lies in the oppo-
sition between those in whom the sensual
principle is regnant and those in whom
the spiritual principle is regnant, and in
the inward struggle of the noble heart
against the evil, and of the sinful heart
against the good."[1] Such a conflict, —
such a struggle, — is a *moral* one. It
involves moral choice, and moral endeavor.
It is a matter of will, which means, as previously stated, free-will.

[1] H. Van Dyke, The Poetry of Tennyson, 10th ed.,
N. Y. 1898, pp. 198, 199.

In *De Profundis*, a poem inspired by
the birth of the poet's grandson, we have
" the abysmal deeps of personality "
dwelt upon. He refers to the soul's pre-
existence, incarnation, nature, and destiny.
Its nature is a profound mystery. It is the
miracle of miracles. It is of the Infinite,
yet distinct from the Infinite. Of it we
may say, "Thou art thou." It has a
being-for-self. It has the power of deter-
mining its own action, and of action upon
things : —

> "who wrought
> Not Matter, nor the finite-infinite,
> But this main-miracle, that thou art thou,
> With power on thine own act and on the world."

Here freedom is affirmed. Self-determination is regarded as of the very constitution of that main-miracle of personality ;
— of that being " which has the power to
feel 'I am I.' "

In the poem *Despair*, Tennyson enters
a protest against both ultra-theological and
agnostic conceptions of God and life.

According to the words prefixed to the poem, it is based on the following incident: "A man and his wife having lost faith in a God, and hope of a life to come, and being utterly miserable in this, resolve to end themselves by drowning. The woman is drowned, but the man rescued by a minister of the sect he had abandoned." The man almost curses the minister for rescuing him, and, in his remonstrance, gives reasons for his conduct and that of his wife. The bitter experiences of life drove them to despair. They could derive no comfort or encouragement from the conceptions of God, and man's relation to Him, presented in the theology of the sect to which they had belonged. This theology was a creed of *Fatalism*, —

"See, we were nursed in the drear night-fold of
    your fatalist creed."

Such a "fatalist creed" gives us a God of cruelty rather than a God of love, for he creates us, foreknows us, and *foredooms* us, and *does with us as he will.* —

"What! I should call on that Infinite Love that
       has served us so well?
Infinite cruelty rather that made everlasting Hell,
Made us, foreknew us, foredoom'd us, and does
       what he will with his own;
Better our dead brute mother who never has
       heard us groan!"

The outcome of such teaching is, a
rejection of belief in a personal God, and
in the reality and immortality of the soul.
"Bawling" the dark side of the preach-
er's faith flings these two back on themselves, "the human heart, and the Age."
But no hope or comfort is to be derived
from the age, with its "horrible infidel
writings," and its "know-nothing books."
The times are "the new-dark ages," and
doubt is "the lord of this dunghill."

It is evident, then, that one of the things
against which the poet is protesting in this
poem is, the views of human freedom em-
bodied in the dogmas of foreknowledge and
foreordination of the "know-all chapel"
with its "know-all" creed. These views
cancel freedom, they constitute a "fatalist

creed." Not only does the poem reveal this, but it is corroborated by external evidence. As we have already seen, he wrote at the end of the poem the words: " In my boyhood I came across the Calvinist Creed, and assuredly however unfathomable the mystery, if one cannot believe in the freedom of the human will as of the Divine, life is hardly worth having." In short, the import of Tennyson's protest against fatalism as revealed in this poem is, that belief in freedom is essential to a conception of the worth of life.

Turning next to *The Ancient Sage*, we find freedom recognised at least by implication. We have already seen that this speculative poem deals with materialistic and agnostic views of God and immortality. These conceptions are represented by a youth, who, in a " scroll of verse," also gives expression to pessimistic views of human life which naturally follow such conceptions of God and destiny. The sage (who represents the views of the poet) re-

plies to the youth, that human life is a trust
put into our keeping, for which we are
responsible, and enjoins the youth, despite
the dark side to life, and indeed, because
of it, to a noble life of self-control, and
service to our fellow-men, which lies within
the sphere of choice or self-determination.
In response to the words of the youth, —

> " And Night and Shadow rule below
>   When only day should reign,"

the sage says that if there were no night
there would be no day, — no evil, there
would be no good; but that —

> " night enough is there
> In yon dark city: get thee back: and since
> The key to that weird casket, which for thee
> But holds a skull, is neither thine nor mine,
> But in the hand of what is more than man,
> Or in man's hand when man is more than man,
> Let be thy wail and help thy fellow men,
> And make thy gold thy vassal not thy king,
> And fling free alms into the beggar's bowl,
> And send the day into the darken'd heart;
> Nor list for guerdon in the voice of men,
> A dying echo from a falling wall;

Nor care — for Hunger hath the Evil eye —
To vex the noon with fiery gems, or fold
Thy presence in the silk of sumptuous looms;
Nor roll thy viands on a luscious tongue,
Nor drown thyself with flies in honied wine;
Nor thou be rageful, like a handled bee,
And lose thy life by usage of thy sting ;
Nor harm an adder thro' the lust for harm,
Nor make a snail's horn shrink for wantonness ;
And more — think well ! Do-well will follow
    thought,
And in the fatal sequence of this world
An evil thought may soil thy children's blood;
But curb the beast would cast thee in the mire,
And leave the hot swamp of voluptuousness
A cloud between the Nameless and thyself,
And lay thine uphill shoulder to the wheel,
And climb the Mount of Blessing," etc.

In these words we have a clear call to a moral choice, to a moral decision, to moral self-control, to moral achievement, to moral service to self and others. Such a call involves a recognition of freedom.

In *Locksley Hall Sixty Years After*, we find another declaration of the reality of freedom. Man is enjoined to —

" Follow Light, and do the Right — for man can
    half-control his doom, — "

which words remind us of the more emphatic words to the same effect, recorded in *The Marriage of Geraint:*—

"For man is man and master of his fate."

The Promise of May is a poem of ethical import.[1] It was written with the purpose of pointing out the tendencies of materialistic Agnosticism,—especially as manifest in human character and conduct. It is a story of illicit love, in which Edgar (afterwards known as Harold) is the representative in belief and practice of the agnostic "creed." With him virtue is not a reality.

[1] This play was produced at the Globe Theatre, November 11, 1882, under the direction of Mrs. Bernard-Beere. It was a complete failure. On the night of November 14th of the same year, as the piece was nearing the close of the first act, the Marquis of Queensbury sprang to his feet exclaiming, "I beg to protest . . ."; but adding, "I will wait till the end of the act," he returned to his seat. When the curtain had fallen he again stood up, and, confessing himself an agnostic, declared that Tennyson's Edgar was an 'abominable caricature' into whose mouth the poet had put sentiments that did not exist among free thinkers. — MORTON LUCE, *A Handbook to the Works of Alfred Lord Tennyson*, pp. 411, 412.   Cf. Memoir, vol. ii., pp. 266-269.

There is no essential distinction between
virtue and vice.   He says:—

> " one time's vice may be
> The virtue of another; and Vice and Virtue
> Are but two masks of self; and what hereafter
> Shall mark out Vice from Virtue in the gulf
> Of never-dawning darkness."

So-called morals are merely slavish cus-
toms and conventionalities.   " The morals
of the tribe " are simply the " swaddling-
bands" of man, which, as " the child of
evolution," he will " fling aside " as he
moves on to a life not higher than, but in
conformity to, Nature.   Free-will,—

> "the crowd would call it conscience "—

is a misnomer.   The *reality* is, that we are
determined by " the stronger motive."
Man is merely—

> " A willy-nilly current of sensations."

This is Edgar's creed, and, as put in
practice by him, results in moral disaster.
Tennyson's purpose seems to be, to protest
against such a creed from the standpoint
of its practical consequences.   To make

man a mere child of Nature, governed only by mechanical laws, subject to the strongest motive, — cancels morality, and reduces man to mere animalism. Such a conception of man makes Nature a liar, for what is the meaning of the moral emotions if man be not responsible for his conduct; and how can he be held responsible for his conduct if he be not free? Tennyson puts the case most forcefully in the words of Edgar: —

> "if man be only
> A willy-nilly current of sensations —
> Reaction needs must follow revel — yet —
> Why feel remorse, he, knowing that he *must* have
> Moved in the iron grooves of Destiny?
> Remorse then is a part of Destiny,
> Nature a liar, making us feel guilty
> Of her own faults."

There are three poems, belonging to the closing years of Tennyson's life, which imply his belief in the reality of freedom. They are entitled, *By an Evolutionist; The Dawn*, and *The Making of Man*. Tennyson believed in organic evolution.

He believed that the human body was descended from a lower form of animal life. However, in his judgment, this is not so of the human soul. It is not an evolution of the brute mind. Men are not "slaves of a four-footed will," but beings of "heaven-descended Will." Now, since man is a compound being, consisting of body and soul, it is the province of man as "heaven-descended Will" to rule over man as animal-descended body. In other words, man as spirit ought to rule himself as body. This involves a severe struggle. The animalism in us is strong. "The flesh warreth against the spirit." But we are moral beings, with moral ideals, possessed of the sovereign power of self-determination, so that it is possible, by a proper exercise of will, to obey the exhortation, —

> "Arise and fly
> The reeling Faun, the sensual feast;
> Move upward, working out the beast,
> And let the ape and tiger die."

7

The soul is to hold the sceptre, and to rule its " Province of the brute." This is undoubtedly the teaching of the first of the poems mentioned above : —

I

"If my body come from brutes, tho' somewhat
      finer than their own,
    I am heir, and this my kingdom, shall the
      royal voice be mute?
No, but if the rebel subject seek to drag me from
      the throne,
    Hold the sceptre, Human Soul, and rule thy
      Province of the brute.

II

"I have climb'd to the snows of Age, and I gaze
      at a field in the Past,
    Where I sank with the body at times in the
      sloughs of a low desire,
But I hear no yelp of the beast, and the Man is
      quiet at last
    As he stands on the heights of his life with
      a glimpse of a height that is higher."

This, too, is the import of the second of the poems referred to above. The last two verses indicate this. Men are not " slaves of a four-footed will;" but there

are degrees of freedom. They have not
attained unto a complete freedom from
the power of their animality. Man in his
moral development has only reached the
dawn, and not the *day ;* but although a few
only have reached a high level in moral
development, we must remember "there
is time for the race to grow." By and by
man will reach the *noon* instead of the
dawn.

" Dawn not Day !

Is it Shame, so few should have climb'd from
the dens in the level below,

Men, with a heart and a soul, no slaves of a
four-footed will ?

But if twenty million of summers are stored
in the sunlight still,

We are far from the noon of man, there is time
for the race to grow."

" Red of dawn !

Is it turning a fainter red ? so be it, but when
shall we lay

The Ghost of the Brute that is walking and
haunting us yet, and be free ?

In a hundred, a thousand winters ? Ah, what
will *our* children be,

The men of a hundred thousand, a million summers away ? "

The last of the three poems referred to above is very similar to the other two in regard to its real import. Man is gradually rising above his bestiality; gradually moving upward from the life of the flesh into the richer life of the spirit. He is slowly " being made "; but ultimately he will be made. But, if we are to interpret these words in accordance with Tennyson's general teaching, " the making of man," is a process of self-making. He is making himself by a proper exertion of his free spirit under Divine guidance.

" Where is one that, born of woman, altogether can escape
 From the lower world within him, moods of tiger, or of ape?
  Man as yet is being made, and ere the crowning Age of ages,
 Shall not aeon after aeon pass and touch him into shape?

" All about him shadow still, but, while the races flower and fade,
 Prophet-eyes may catch a glory slowly gaining on the shade,

Till the peoples all are one, and all their
    voices blend in choric
Hallelujah to the Maker 'It is finished. Man
    is made.'"

But while freedom is a reality, — it is a
progressive reality. There are degrees of
freedom. The more we progress morally,
the freer we become. "Man's Free-will
is but a bird in a cage; he can stop at
the lower perch, or he can mount to a
higher. Then that which is and knows
will enlarge his cage, give him a higher
and a higher perch, and at last break off
the top of his cage, and let him out to
be one with the Free-will of the Universe." [1] In short, Tennyson believed that
free-will is the root of moral character;
that moral character is a development;
that the glory of virtue is —

    " The glory of going on, and still to be;"

that the progressive realisation of the
moral ideal is a progressive realisation of

[1] Memoir, vol. i., pp. 318, 319.

freedom; that this moral development, with its increasing freedom, extends into the immortal life — the dead breathing " an ampler day," "for ever nobler ends." Is this not the teaching of such poems as *Wages*, *In Memoriam*, cxviii., *By an Evolutionist*, *The Dawn*, and *The Making of Man* ?

It is evident, then, that a review of the poetry of Tennyson discloses the fact that he *believed* in the reality of freedom. Let us now endeavor to determine his position with reference to the *knowableness* of the reality. Very early in his career, in *The Poet*, he recognised the marvellous character of the will, although

" The marvel of the everlasting will "

lies before the superior vision of the seer

" An open scroll."

But the will, with Tennyson, is really an unknowable, inexplicable reality. This is quite evident in the prologue to *In Memoriam*. Here, as we have already

seen, he affirms the reality of free-will.
Our wills are ours is the explicit declaration. This declaration is repeated, and a
further affirmation of the fact is given in
the words "to make them thine." That
is, there is a double affirmation of the
reality of free-will in the words,

" Our wills are ours, to make them thine,"

because the power "to make them thine"
is nothing else than the power of self-
determination. But the "how" of self-
determination is unknowable, according
to the poet; for, he says: —

" Our wills are ours, we know not how."

And this unknowableness seems to be re-
affirmed later in the prologue, for it appears to be a justifiable interpretation of
the words of verse 6, —

" We have but faith: we cannot know,"

to apply them to free-will, as well as to
God and immortality — the three subjects
mentioned in the preceding verses.

A similar position is taken by the poet

in *De Profundis*. Personality, of which
self-determination is one of the essential
constituents, is an inconceivable reality, —

"Who made thee unconceivably Thyself."

It is a miracle; indeed, the "main-
miracle," as Tennyson declares in the
words, —

"... who wrought
Not matter, nor the finite-infinite,
But this main-miracle, that thou art thou,
With power on thine own act and on the world."

Meagre as are his words on this subject, are they not sufficient, when taken
in connection with what he has said concerning the reality of free-will, to justify
us in saying, that the poet's position in
regard to freedom is, that it is not a
knowable reality, but a *believable* one. It
is not a fact or truth of the knowing
mind, but of the believing soul, — a reality
concerning which —

"We have but faith : we cannot know."

We believe in it largely on the authority

of the " practical reason," or moral consciousness. It is necessary for the explanation of the moral life; it is necessary
for living the moral life. In short, freedom is a practical or moral postulate.
Tennyson's position here is essentially in
harmony with his " Faith Philosophy,"
as we have been made acquainted with it
in examining what he has said concerning
our knowledge of God. God and freedom
are "unknown and unknowable realities."
They belong to the noumenal, to which the
human mind, through sense and reason,
cannot attain. But, on the other hand,
they are believable realities, — posited by
the believing soul.

IMMORTALITY

Thou wilt not leave us in the dust.
In Memoriam, Prologue, 3

The face of Death is toward the Sun of Life,
His shadow darkens earth : his truer name
Is " Onward ! "
The Death of the Duke of Clarence and Avondale.

IMMANUEL KANT, in the Introduction to his famous *Critique of Pure Reason*, says, that there are certain problems concerning which "reason prosecutes its investigations, which [investigations] by their importance we consider far more excellent and by their tendency far more elevated than anything the understanding can find in the sphere of phenomena. Nay, we risk rather anything, even at the peril of error, than that we should surrender such investigations, either on the ground of their uncertainty, or from any feeling of indifference or contempt." [1] And, in the second edition, he informs us that "these inevitable problems of pure reason itself are, *God*, *Freedom*, and *Immortality*." [2] Of these, the third occupies the most prominent place in Tennyson's reflection. All through his career as a poet, this problem engages his attention. It gives rise to his profoundest thought. It stirs his deepest emotion. It perplexes his sublimest faith. And, in his endeavor to "beat his music out," he gives to the world some of his most consummate art.

The reasons why this problem engages so much of his attention have already been stated. We have found them to be primarily the loss of his friend, Arthur Henry Hallam, and the materialistic and agnostic tendencies of his age. Hallam was a young man of unusual mental endowments

[1] Critique of Pure Reason, trans. by Müller, vol. ii., Int., pp. 2–3.
[2] Ibid., p. 3.

and exceedingly fine character.   Throughout *In Memoriam* Tennyson speaks of him
in the most exalted terms.[1]   His was —

> " A life that all the Muses deck'd
>> With gifts of grace, that might express
>> All-comprehensive tenderness,
> All-subtilising intellect."

His was —

> " High nature amorous of the good,
>> But touch'd with no ascetic gloom."

His was a —

> " manhood fused with female grace."

Indeed, Tennyson says, he was the man he
" held as half-divine."

Between these two young men existed
a peculiarly strong and affectionate friendship.   The poet speaks of him as —

> " Dear as the mother to the son,
> More than my brothers are to me."

as —

> " The human-hearted man I loved."

---

[1] Cf. especially poems LVII., LX., LXXII., LXXIX.,
LXXXIV., LXXXV., LXXXVII., XCVI., XCIX., CIX., CX., CXI.,
CXII., and CXIII.   This exalted opinion Tennyson cher-
ished throughout his life.   It was also entertained, in a
large measure, by the mutual friends of Tennyson and
Hallam.

He also speaks of himself, in his relation to Hallam, as —

> " the divided half of such
> A friendship as had master'd Time."

In 1832, an additional tie was formed between the two friends. Hallam became engaged to Tennyson's sister Emily. The poet refers pathetically to this relation,[1] and its possible outcome as bearing on his own life, had Hallam lived. But the marriage was never to take place. A " remorseless iron hour " was destined to make " cypress of her orange flower," "despair of hope," and earth of Arthur Hallam. In 1833, as "the day was drawing on," while travelling on the Continent, Hallam fell ill with fever, to which he ultimately succumbed. He died in Vienna, September 15, of the same year.

> " My blood an even tenor kept,
>   Till on mine ear this message falls,
>   That in Vienna's fatal halls,
> God's finger touch'd him, and he slept."

[1] In Memoriam, LXXXIV.

Now, the desire, born of the heart's deepest affection, that Love shall " never lose its own," impelled Tennyson to serious reflection on the grounds for believing that it may eternally claim its object. In his reflection, as we have already seen, he had to encounter the spirit of the age, which was, in many respects, anything but encouraging to a would-be believer in immortality. We have noted that the Materialism and Sensationalism of the age cancelled the reality of the soul, and consequently its immortality. Also, that the Agnosticism of the age denied a knowledge of the soul and thereby of its immortality. Again, that the biblical criticism of the times weakened the confidence of many in the authority of the Scriptures; and, as a result, their declarations concerning " the life everlasting " lost much of their force. It was this powerful spirit of doubt and denial which Tennyson had to encounter in trying to establish himself firmly in a belief in man's immortal future. We shall see that for more than half a century he fought his battle; and it is not irreverent to say, that, with both internal and external foes, he fought a good fight; he finished his course, and he kept the faith.

The history of Tennyson's mental attitude toward the question of immortality may be divided into four periods. These are quite distinguishable, both logically and chronologically. The first, may be called the period of naïve, uncritical belief, in which the poet rests in the undisturbed confidence of an inherited faith. The second, is when he awakes from the sleep of dogmatism and experiences the first rude shocks of doubt. The third, finds him engaged in a reflective consideration of the question, endeavoring to establish his faith on a rational basis in the face of his own doubts and those of his age. The fourth, finds him emerging from this long period of rational consideration, into the enjoyment of a calm and serene faith.

The first period — that of naïve, uncritical belief — is the period in which things
are believed on the authority of parent,
society, and the church. No rational
ground for their acceptance is demanded
— indeed, hardly dreamed of as necessary. The body of supposed religious
truth is received as a matter of course.
He, like thousands of others, is, so to
speak, born into them. His father was
a Christian minister. His mother was a
woman of simple and earnest Christian
faith. He was born and reared in a
Christian land. In other words, his envi-
ronment was Christian. He merely ex-
emplified human nature in receiving the
creed of his parents, church, and country,
at first, with most unquestioning faith.
This is the period in which the native
dogmatism of the mind still rules. Reflection has not yet awakened it from its
" dogmatic slumber." This simple attitude toward the question is noticeable in
the earliest poetry of Tennyson as found

in *Poems, by Two Brothers*[1] — published by
Charles Turner Tennyson and his brother
Alfred, when the former was eighteen,
and the latter fifteen, years of age.   There
are several poems in this volume which
touch upon the subject of immortality.
One of these, credited to Alfred Tennyson, is entitled : *Why should we Weep
for Those who Die ?*   It reads as follows :

> " Why should we weep for those who die ?
>   They fall — their dust returns to dust ;
>   Their souls shall live eternally
>   Within the mansions of the just.
>
> " They die to live — they sink to rise,
>   They leave this wretched mortal shore ;
>   But brighter suns and bluer skies
>   Shall smile on them for evermore.
>
> " Why should we sorrow for the dead ?
>   Our life on earth is but a span ;
>   They tread the path that all must tread,
>   They die the common death of man.

[1] Poems, by Two Brothers.   London : Printed for
W. Simpkin and R. Marshall, Stationers'-Hall-Court ;
and J. and J. Jackson, Louth. MDCCCXXVII.   Copies
of this edition are very rare.   A second edition was
published by Macmillan & Co., New York and London,
1893.

" The noblest songster of the gale
  Must cease, when Winter's frowns appear;
The reddest rose is wan and pale,
  When Autumn tints the changing year.

The fairest flower on earth must fade,
  The brightest hopes on earth must die:
Why should we mourn that man was made
  To droop on earth, but dwell on high?

" The soul, th' eternal soul must reign
  In worlds devoid of pain and strife;
Then why should mortal man complain
  Of death, which leads to happier life? "

No questioning here as to whether " death
ends all." He knows nothing here of the
"sunless gulfs of doubt." No voice has
yet murmured —

              " from the narrow house,
    The cheeks drop in; the body bows;
  Man dies: nor is there hope in dust."

It is the spring-time of faith. Nothing
but promise is seen in anything — even in
death.

Another poem of this early period,
which illustrates this simple, untainted
faith, is entitled *Remorse*. In the pre-

ceding poem it is apparent that it is simple Christian faith which is expressed; and it is the happy side of Christian faith — the immortality which awaits the just. In this second poem he again gives expression to his inherited Christian beliefs in the future life. Here, however, his faith embodies itself in ultra-theological views of the punishment which awaits the wicked after death. The poem describes the mental state of an old man as he reflects upon a misspent life, and the penalty which the future life will bring. After calling attention to the mental pictures which arise when reviewing such a life, he contemplates the present and future.

> " If I am damn'd, why find I not
>   Some comfort in this earthly spot?
>   But no! this world and that to come
>   Are both to me one scene of gloom !
>   .   .   .   .
>
>   And I was cursed from my birth,
>   A reptile made to creep on earth,
>   An hopeless outcast, born to die
>   A living death eternally !
>   With too much conscience to have rest,

> Too little to be ever blest,
> To yon vast world of endless woe
>   Unlighted by the cheerful day,
>   My soul shall wing her weary way;
>   To those dread depths where aye the same,
> Throughout the waste of darkness, glow
>   The glimmerings of the boundless flame."

Despite his misery in this world he still clings to it —

>   " . . . for well
>   I know the pangs that rack me now
>   Are trifles, to the endless hell
>   That waits me, when my burning brow
>   And my wrung eyes shall hope in vain
>   For one small drop to cool the pain,
>   The fury of that madd'ning flame
>   That then shall scorch my writhing frame!

>   .   .   .   .

> " Oh, God ! that thou wouldst grant that ne'er
>   My soul its clay-cold bed forsake,
>   That I might sleep, and never wake
> Unto the thrill of conscious fear ;
>   For when the trumpet's piercing cry
> Shall burst upon my slumb'ring ear,
>   And countless seraphs throng the sky,
> How shall I cast my shroud away,
> And come into the blaze of day ?
> How shall I brook to hear each crime,
> Here veil'd by secrecy and time,

Read out from thine eternal book?
How shall I stand before thy throne,
While earth shall like a furnace burn?
How shall I bear the with'ring look
Of men and angels, who will turn
Their dreadful gaze on me alone?"

In this poem, even after making allowance for metaphor and "poetic license," we have the most realistic conceptions of future punishment, — an exaggerated interpretation of extreme theological views. Some men are born to an eternal living death. The pangs of earth are trifles to what awaits those who are doomed to an endless and hopeless hell. There will be a naked revelation of crimes that have here been "veil'd by secrecy and time." Absolute death is more to be preferred than to awake to "the thrill of conscious fear" of an impending doom. All of this indicates that Tennyson is giving expression to an unexamined, unquestioned, inherited faith on the subject of the immortal destiny of the wicked. So that these two poems plainly show his first attitude

toward the question of immortality to be
one of naïve credence, — of simple, unquestioning, dogmatic belief.

And now we come to the second period
of his mental history concerning this great
question. But how widely different in
character it is! Faith has received its
first rude encounter. The mind has been
awakened from its "dogmatic slumber."
It asks itself the question whether, after
all, these things which seemed so profoundly real, were not merely the dreams
of the soul in the sleep of dogmatism.
The rosy visions of youthful faith are
gone. "The spectres of the mind" have
taken their place, and, in wretchedness
of soul, he is trying to "lay them." He
has entered upon the reflective period of
life, and the penalty is disquietude of spirit.
This period probably dawned during his
university career, and was the result of
gradually maturing mind, and increasing
knowledge, as well as contact with the
conflicting opinion and doubt of the age.

The change in Tennyson is profound, and the effect on his sensitive soul is easily discerned in a poem, composed at this time, entitled *Supposed Confessions of a Second-Rate Sensitive Mind.* It is an exceedingly pathetic utterance, — the cry of a soul bruised and torn by a hand-to-hand conflict with Doubt. An analysis of the poem will reveal the severity of the struggle, as well as the gloom and despair which have taken possession of his soul.

It opens with a prayer to God for mercy in his wretched condition. He reproaches himself in this prayer because, despite God's love manifest in the sufferings and death of Christ, there is need of something more to strengthen his belief; and for thinking a visible sign might avail him in this respect. After a description of his misery, he breaks forth in an exclamation in which is revealed the fact, that it is the question of immortality concerning which he is especially in doubt. He says : —

" How sweet to have a common faith !
  To hold a common scorn of death !
  And at a burial to hear
  The creaking cords which wound and eat
  Into my human heart, whene'er
  Earth goes to earth, with grief, not fear,
  With hopeful grief, were passing sweet ! "

But apparently this faith and " hopeful grief " are not his. There is longing for the " thrice happy state " of the " trustful infant." There is yearning for the spiritual quietude of his mother which, as a child, he discerned as he bowed at her knee and listened to her vows in prayer for him. Why is it that we get away from such influences ? What devil had the heart to ruthlessly destroy the flowers of faith which she had reared? Is he himself that devil? But why have her prayers for him not availed, for she was " great in faith "? What use in praying to a God who does not hear; or if he hear, does not heed? These are the questions he raises, and the reflections involved distract him.

" Why not believe then ? Why not yet
    Anchor thy frailty there, where man
    Hath moor'd and rested ? "

But the utter hopelessness of his condition
manifests itself in the answer he gives to
his own question.   Why not believe?
Why not anchor my frailty there?

                        " Ask the sea
    At midnight, when the crisp slope waves
    After a tempest, rib and fret
    The broad-imbased beach, why he
    Slumbers not like a mountain tarn ?
    Wherefore his ridges are not curls
    And ripples of an inland mere ?
    Wherefore he moaneth thus, nor can
    Draw down into his vexed pools
    All that blue heaven which hues and paves
    The other ? "

As such behavior is impossible for the
sea, so belief is impossible for him.   He is
" forlorn " and " shaken ; " his own weakness fools his judgment, and his spirit —

                        " whirls
    " Moved from beneath with doubt and fear."

And now the poet, representing himself
as having passed the period of youth, re-

fers to the confident air with which in
youth he went forth in the pursuit of truth;
and how he then justified his doubt on the
grounds that it was a means to a noble
end, — the firmer establishment of truth.
Furthermore, the animal lives from moment to moment, with no fear or suspicion
even that life will not continue. But shall
man, a rational, investigating mind, live
thus? Rather —

> " Shall we not look into the laws
>   Of life and death, and things that seem,
>   And things that be, and analyse
>   Our double nature, and compare
>   All creeds till we have found the one,
>   If one there be ? "

However well this may sound, our poet
soon becomes conscious of the fact that it
is not a safe course for all to pursue, himself included, — at least at this period of his
career, — and, in his wretchedness, he calls
upon God for light.

> " Ay me ! I fear
>   All may not doubt, but everywhere
>   Some must clasp Idols. Yet, my God,

Whom call I Idol?   Let Thy dove
Shadow me over, and my sins
Be unremember'd, and Thy love
Enlighten me.   Oh teach me yet
Somewhat before the heavy clod
Weighs on me, and the busy fret
Of that sharp-headed worm begins
In the gross blackness underneath."

His prayer, however, fails to bring relief.
He is left betwixt doubt and belief and
does not know which way to turn.   The
extreme wretchedness of his state of mind is
expressed in the final words of the poem:

"O weary life!   O weary death!
O spirit and heart made desolate!
O damned vacillating state!"

This poem is undoubtedly a history of
Tennyson's own mental struggle with
doubt concerning the fundamental problems of thought and life.   More especially, as he intimates, it represents his
struggle with reference to the problem of
immortality.   It is a fair description of the
experience peculiar to the mind as it
leaves the period of authority and unques-

tioning belief and enters upon the period
of reflection, in which it endeavors to
rationalise its faith, — in which it seeks " to
give a reason for the faith " that is within
it.   This often constitutes a crisis in the
life of the soul.   Two ways out of it usually
reveal themselves.   Refuge may be taken
in authority, — putting an end to all questioning, and resting in a blind faith.   Or,
on the other hand, as Tennyson himself
describes it, to refuse to make the judgment blind, — to face " the spectres of the
mind," and lay them.   Tennyson adopted
the latter course.   The adoption and carry-
ing out of this course brings us to the
third period in the development of his
attitude toward the problem of immortality.
This period is one of rational inquiry
into the grounds of belief.   Serious doubts
concerning it having arisen, — fortified by
the scientific investigations and reflective
thought of the age, — it was necessary for
him to make an examination of the subject
in the light of what science and philosophy

had to say. The necessity for a personal investigation of the question, as before stated, seems to have dawned on him in connection with the death of his much-beloved friend, Arthur Hallam. Death usually raises the question of immortality in a reflective mind; and, as previously suggested, the claims of Love to everlasting possession of its object, specially impel man to consider it. But we misinterpret Tennyson if we make his own satisfaction and peace of mind the only motive prompting him to this inquiry. He realised before he had reflected long, that his cry was but an echo of the great cry of the human heart; that his question was its question; and that his answer might possibly be its answer. This conviction soon became an inspiring motive to an earnest inquiry; and herein do we specially see its ethical significance. Let us now trace the development of this third period.[1]

[1] It is not meant, that throughout this period there was a non-committal attitude, — an attitude of mere con-

The first evidence of such rational consideration of the subject revealed by his
poetry is found in a poem entitled *The
Two Voices.*[1]   This is a philosophical
poem.   Its real subject is, "The Worth of
Life."   It consists of a series of arguments
and counter-arguments in which the pros

sideration of pros and cons. Sometimes, we find him
in great perplexity of mind; sometimes, in doubt and
despair; again, apparently well-grounded in faith. But
the essential point is, that during this period of more
than fifty years the subject is under rational consideration. He endeavors to determine the grounds of
belief in immortality, and to proclaim and rationally
defend the Faith. This long period may, in a sense,
be divided into two. The first, in which he specially
struggles with his own doubts, suggested in a measure,
and strengthened, by the doubts of his age. This closes
with *In Memoriam*, in the prologue of which he strikes
a note of triumph —

    "Thou wilt not leave us in the dust."

The second, is subsequent to *In Memoriam*, in which
he deals more especially with the doubts of his age,
endeavoring to make a rational defence of his belief,
realising all of the time its vital importance as bearing
on human life. However, this division must not be regarded too literally.

[1] First published in the volume entitled *English Idylls
and Other Poems*, 1842. It then bore the date of 1833,
which, however, was removed afterward.

and cons are skilfully presented. The
worthlessness of life, and the advantages
of suicide as a remedy for life's ills, are
represented by a tempting voice. The
value of life, and the obligation to maintain it, are represented by the subject
tempted. After the controversy, a voice
that "sees the end," "and knows the
good," whispers the Christian view of life.

In the course of the discussion the poet,
Hamlet-like, raises the question, whether,
after all, death would put an end to misery.
It might simply be a means of going from
bad to worse. —

> "I toil beneath the curse,
>   But, knowing not the universe,
>   I fear to slide from bad to worse."

This apprehension brings the subject of
immortality into the discussion, and, as a
result, we have quite an elaborate argument for and against belief in man's immortal future. The first voice presents,
with considerable force, the evidence from
sense against it. So far as we can observe

by the senses, the dead give no evidence of life. The face of the dead man is expressionless. It gives no indication of "passion, pain, or pride." Neither is there response to a command. No answer to a grasp of the hand. Smite him on the cheek and mouth, and he speaks not. —

> "There is no other thing express'd
>   But long disquiet merged in rest."

Indeed, the things in life which would most concern him, affect him not: —

> "His little daughter, whose sweet face
>   He kiss'd, taking his last embrace,
>   Becomes dishonour to her race —

> "His sons grow up that bear his name,
>   Some grow to honour, some to shame, —
>   But he is chill to praise or blame."

Absolute indifference to all things cosmic and human is his state.

This argument from sense, however, does not appeal to the poet as conclusive. He wants to know —

> "Why, if man rot in dreamless ease,
>   Should that plain fact, as taught by these,
>   Not make him sure that he shall cease?

> " Who forged that other influence
> That heat of inward evidence,
> By which he doubts against the sense ? "

This " inward evidence " of spirit must be set over against the outward evidence of sense. As a matter of fact, although man reads his body " as a thing that dies," he reads his spirit differently. He reads it as an entity surviving death. —

> " He owns the fatal gift of eyes,
> That read his spirit blindly wise,
> Not simple as a thing that dies."

Man's aspirations reach beyond Time. In his heart are the forebodings of a great mystery. In his mind is the concept of Eternity. —

> " Here sits he shaping wings to fly:
> His heart forebodes a mystery:
> He names the name Eternity."

Again, he is richly endowed. He is a religious, rational, and moral being. He has an ideal of the Perfect. Nowhere in Nature is it actualised. Does it carry us beyond Nature to the Supernatural?

9

He is a being who has conceptions of God and of his relations to Him; who can reflect on his own origin and destiny; who has ideals of moral worth, and can impose them upon himself as laws of conduct; a being " so God-like in faculty," must have a nobler destiny than the dust.—

> " That type of Perfect in his mind
>   In Nature can he nowhere find,
>   He sows himself on every wind."

> " He seems to hear a Heavenly Friend,
>   And thro' thick veils to apprehend
>   A labour working to an end.

> " The end and the beginning vex
>   His reason: many things perplex,
>   With motions, checks, and counterchecks.

> " He knows a baseness in his blood
>   At such strange war with something good,
>   He may not do the thing he would."

Furthermore, man has a kind of spiritual vision of the immortal life: —

> " Heaven opens inward, chasms yawn,
>   Vast images in glimmering dawn,
>   Half shown, are broken and withdrawn."

All of this constitutes the "inward evidence" of spirit which leads man to doubt the outward evidence of sense. The poet thinks the unbeliever slain by his own weapon, — Doubt; that the fact that man doubts against the outward evidence of sense, constitutes a pre-supposition in favor of belief in immortality.

But the unbeliever resumes. There is other evidence which makes against belief in immortality. "To begin, implies to end." Man has had a beginning; he must, therefore, have an end. Whatever force this thesis may have, — and the poet thinks it has very little, — is offset, in his judgment, by the intimations which man has of his pre-existence, — that he was not, at least, first cast "in human mould." This is merely dreaming and not argument to the sceptic, and he shrewdly calls attention to the main question under consideration — The Worth of Life — by pointing to something which is not a dream but a reality. —

>   " ' I talk,' said he,
> ' Not with thy dreams. Suffice it thee
> Thy pain is a reality.' "

The poet, however, is not convinced by the gloomy representations of the unbelieving voice that life is not worth living, and closes the discussion with the affirmation of a fact which is regarded by many as constituting one of the strongest grounds for belief in the soul's immortality; namely, that it is not death, but *life* — larger, fuller, completer life — which man desires. —

> " Whatever crazy sorrow saith,
> No life that breathes with human breath
> Has ever truly long'd for death.

> " T is life, whereof our nerves are scant,
> Oh life, not death, for which we pant;
> More life, and fuller, that I want."

Some light on the subjective or personal character of this poem may be gained from the following words contained in the *Memoir*: [1] "When I wrote *The Two*

---

[1] Vol. i. p. 193 n.

Voices," says Tennyson to his son, " I was utterly miserable, a burden to myself and to my family, that I said, 'Is life worth anything?'" We have seen above what a conspicuous place immortality occupies in his answer to the question raised; hence, undoubtedly, the earnest consideration of the subject which this poem reveals.

The next evidence of such rational consideration of the question in his poetry, is found in *In Memoriam*. Very naturally we expect to find the fullest development of his thought here; and, indeed, a careful examination of this great work brings no disappointment in this respect. We find here the same consideration of the pros and cons which is manifest in *The Two Voices*, but the reflection is more profound.

Tennyson himself has explained the nature of the poem. He said: "It must be remembered that this is a poem, *not* an actual biography. It is founded on our friendship, on the engagement of Arthur

Hallam to my sister, on his sudden death at Vienna, just before the time fixed for their marriage, and on his burial at Clevedon Church. The poem concludes with the marriage of my youngest sister Cecilia. It was meant to be a kind of *Divina Commedia*, ending with happiness. The sections were written at many different places, and as the phases of our intercourse came to my memory and suggested them. I did not write them with any view of weaving them into a whole, or for publication, until I found that I had written so many. The different moods of sorrow as in a drama are dramatically given, and my conviction that fear, doubts, and suffering will find answer and relief only through Faith in a God of Love."[1]

The reflective consideration of the question of immortality in *In Memoriam* begins with poems XXXIV.-XXXV.[2] Here the

[1] Memoir, vol. i. pp. 304, 305.

[2] It is very difficult, if not, indeed, impossible, to determine the chronological order of the poems of *In Memoriam*. Their composition covers a period

poet affirms immortality to be an inference
based upon human life itself. If life is to
be crowned by death, if it is not to " live
for evermore," then earth is a dark and
meaningless affair. This is the teaching
of life itself. —

> " My own dim life should teach me this,
> That life shall live for evermore,
> Else earth is darkness at the core,
> And dust and ashes all that is ;
>
> " This round of green, this orb of flame,
> Fantastic beauty ; such as lurks
> In some wild Poet, when he works
> Without a conscience or an aim."

Such a conception or supposition as this
means a Godless world, and this means
the collapse of the religious nature, — the
destruction of religious ideals. With an
earth that is " darkness at the core," whose
beauty is " fantastic " rather than rational ;
with " dust and ashes all that is," what
does " God " mean to the human soul?
This is why the poet asks the question, —

> " What then were God to such as I ? "

of seventeen years. In the above treatment the usual
order of the poems has been followed.

Furthermore, this means the worthlessness of life itself. Mortal things are hardly worth the choosing. The virtue of patience, even in a small measure, is not worth exercising. Indeed, life is really not worth living, — it were better, at once, to cease to be. —

> " 'T were hardly worth my while to choose
>   Of things all mortal, or to use
> A little patience ere I die;

> " 'T were best at once to sink to peace,
>   Like birds the charming serpent draws,
>   To drop head-foremost in the jaws
> Of vacant darkness and to cease."

Again, Love were an impossibility, if death were seen at first merely as death. Or, if possible, it would be an exceedingly poor, narrow, sluggish, and coarse affair, scarcely rising above brutish passion. This, to the poet, is an important consideration. He puts the case thus: Suppose " some voice that man could trust " would tell him that death means extinction. Still it might be said, that it is worth while even here to strive "to keep so sweet a thing" as Love alive. But consciousness of the mortality of Love as involved in his own mortality would lessen its sweetness. It would become even in life a "half-dead" affair. He then adds : —

> " O me, what profits it to put
>   An idle case ?   If Death were seen
>   At first as Death, Love had not been,
> Or been in narrowest working shut,

> " Mere fellowship of sluggish moods,
>   Or in his coarsest Satyr-shape
>   Had bruised the herb and crush'd the grape,
> And bask'd and batten'd in the woods."

After numerous indications of his faith in immortality in various poems of *In Memoriam* [1] which follow those just considered, we meet again with a rational consideration of the subject in poems LIV., LV., and LVI.   Here we have a supreme struggle in which the poet sum-

[1] Poems XXXVIII., XL., XLI., XLII., XLIII., XLIV., XLV., XLVI., XLVII., L., LI., LII.

mons his best energies. He reveals to us the fact that he has been considering the destiny of man in the light of Nature. Tennyson looked at Nature usually through the eyes of Science. He describes his age as one —

> " When Science reaches forth her arms
>   To feel from world to world, and charms
> Her secret from the latest moon."

Probably she can feel her way into the dark " valley of the shadow of death," and charm the secret of the grave. It may be that she can give an answer to the great question, " If a man die, shall he live again ? " So he turns to Nature, and makes his appeal. He reflects upon —

> " The wish, that of the living whole
>   No life may fail beyond the grave,"

and asks whether it may not be traced to the divine in man, —

> " The likest God within the soul."

But inquiring of Nature, he finds her testimony not to be in harmony with this wish. Her story is one of destruction and death, and thus gives rise to the suspicion of a conflict between God and herself. She, indeed, seems to be " careful of the type," but indifferent to, or " careless of the single life." Often, of fifty attempts at fruitage, only one succeeds. Death thwarts the others. Such wholesale destruction and apparent waste are appalling to the poet. They cause him to falter where he firmly trod. This divine wish that —

> " No life shall fail beyond the grave,"

gets no support from Nature; nay, the evidence which she furnishes is overwhelmingly against it. So he comes to the conclusion that the question which he has raised is really too large for human reason. All that he can do is " to stretch lame hands of faith." —

> " The wish, that of the living whole
> No life may fail beyond the grave,
> Derives it not from what we have
> The likest God within the soul?

" Are God and Nature then at strife,
   That Nature lends such evil dreams ?
   So careful of the type she seems,
  So careless of the single life ;

"That I, considering everywhere
   Her secret meaning in her deeds,
   And finding that of fifty seeds
  She often brings but one to bear,

"I falter where I firmly trod,
   And falling with my weight of cares
   Upon the great world's altar-stairs
  That slope thro' darkness up to God,

"I stretch lame hands of faith, and grope,
   And gather dust and chaff, and call
   To what I feel is Lord of all,
  And faintly trust the larger hope."

But he decides to inquire further of Nature on this important subject. As a matter of fact, she is "careless of the single life;" but it is said she is "careful of the type." But is this really so? The statement hardly seems to be substantiated by the evidence. The facts rather indicate the contrary. Nature is even careless of the type; for —

> " From scarped cliff and quarried stone
> She cries, ' A thousand types are gone :
> I care for nothing, all shall go.' "

No immortality of the individual; no immortality of the species. This seems to be the teaching of Nature. So far as this throws light on human immortality, it strongly indicates the improbability of either a personal or race immortality. And, as though this answer of Nature were not sufficiently sweeping, she continues mercilessly : —

> " ' Thou makest thine appeal to me :
> I bring to life, I bring to death :
> The spirit does but mean the breath :
> I know no more.' "

But, discouraging as is this response to his appeal, the poet is loath to let the matter rest here. He is not satisfied. All that Nature has revealed thus far in her answer to his inquiry may be true of other beings, but is it true of man — her last and supreme work — so wonderful in nature and achievement? Is this all that

science can say of the destiny of a being who stands on the very summit of
creation; whose eyes glow with "splendid purpose;" whose powerful religious
instincts impel him to "roll the psalm"
even "to wintry skies," — to put his
trust in God as Love, and in Love as
God's law, despite the fact that Nature,
red with the blood of the conflict of
ages, shrieks against his creed? Is this
all that science can say of the destiny of
him who loves and suffers; who has
moral ideals, and battles "for the True,
the Just?" Is it possible that such a
being — so exalted in creation, so dignified in being, so noble in endeavor —
has no other destiny than to —

> "Be blown about the desert dust,
> Or seal'd within the iron hills"?

If so, then, indeed, is man "a monster,"
"a discord;" then, too, is life as "futile"
as it is "frail." The words of the poet are
very earnest and impressive, revealing

how profoundly interested in, and how deeply he feels, concerning Nature's response to his important appeal. —

"'So careful of the type?' but no.
From scarped cliff and quarried stone
She cries, 'A thousand types are gone:
I care for nothing, all shall go.

"'Thou makest thine appeal to me:
I bring to life, I bring to death:
The spirit does but mean the breath:
I know no more.' And he, shall he,

"Man, her last work, who seem'd so fair,
Such splendid purpose in his eyes,
Who roll'd the psalm to wintry skies,
Who built him fanes of fruitless prayer,

"Who trusted God was love indeed
And love Creation's final law —
Tho' Nature, red in truth and claw
With ravine, shriek'd against his creed —

"Who loved, who suffer'd countless ills,
Who battled for the True, the Just,
Be blown about the desert dust,
Or seal'd within the iron hills?

"No more? A monster then, a dream,
A discord. Dragons of the prime,
That tear each other in their slime,
Were mellow music match'd with him.

"O life as futile, then, as frail!
      O for thy voice to soothe and bless!
      What hope of answer, or redress?
   Behind the veil, behind the veil."

Passing now to poem LXXXII.,[1] we find the poet reflecting again upon the subject of human immortality. We have here a presentation of at least a quasi-argument for belief in the future life. There is an "Eternal Process," and man is involved in it. Death does not stop the onward march of the spirit. It is rather a means of furthering its progress. The body, of course, is mortal, and returns to dust. But these remains are but "the shatter'd stalks" or "ruin'd chrysalis" of a being progressing from state to state. Death may bear —

   "The use of virtue out of earth:"

but the poet knows that —

      "transplanted human worth
      Will bloom to profit, otherwhere."

[1] Poems LX., LXI., LXII., LXIII., LXIV., LXV., LXVI., LXXV., and LXXXI., indicate belief in immortality.

Poem CXVIII.,[1] presents a new phase of the old argument based on the dignity of human nature, and its place in creation. The law of "the solid earth's" formation has been the law of evolution — the law of progress from the lower to the higher, until at last "arose the man;" who, if he typify this great law of Time, is himself not only —

"The herald of a higher race,"

but also —

"of himself in higher place."

When we remember this great progressive movement of Nature, and that man is involved in it, we must believe in the immortality of human love and truth; that the dead "breathe an ampler day," "for ever nobler ends."

And now we find the poet considering the argument against belief in immortality. In three poems he reveals his reflections

---

[1] Poems LXXXIV., LXXXV., XC., XCI., XCII., XCIII., XCIV., XCV., CXVI., and CXVII., are indicative of belief in immortality.

upon the claims of Materialism, Pantheism, and one form of the argument from Sense. In poem CXX., he deals with Materialism. Materialistic science denies the reality of a distinct entity or agent called the mind or soul. All psychic activity is really, in the final analysis, merely a higher form of cerebral activity. All mind activity is brain activity. Hence, ultimately considered, we are merely "cunning casts in clay." The conclusion is evident and inevitable. When death breaks these casts, only unformed clay remains. From unformed clay we came; of organized clay we are; to disorganized clay we return. This, undoubtedly, is Tennyson's interpretation of the view of man taken by materialistic science. Unfortunately, he does not meet these views in his wonted manner. In the Introduction, attention was called to the fact of his unwillingness to "make his judgment blind." Here, however, we find an instance of deviation from his customary attitude of mind. Science may *prove* this materialistic conception of the origin and nature of man, with its necessary implications concerning his destiny. But that makes no difference to our poet; he is resolved to take a higher view, in spite of proof to the contrary. It is one of the very few instances in all of Tennyson's reflections, as revealed by his poetry, in which he manifests a willingness to take refuge in blind faith.[1] He says : —

" I trust I have not wasted breath :
　　I think we are not wholly brain,
　　Magnetic mockeries ; not in vain,
　Like Paul with beasts, I fought with Death ;

" Not only cunning casts in clay :
　　Let Science prove we are, and then
　　What matters Science unto men,
　At least to me ? I would not stay.

" Let him, the wiser man who springs
　　Hereafter, up from childhood shape
　　His action like the greater ape,
　But I was *born* to other things."

[1] Another instance may be found in poem CXXIV., 3, 4.

As in the preceding poem, so in poem CXXIII., we find him reflecting on the evidence which makes against an immortal future for man. Here, as in *The Two Voices*, only in different form, it is the testimony of sense. It is the great fact of change. Everything changes and seems to come to naught. He considers this perishable nature of things in its bearing upon belief in the imperishable nature of the soul. Does it not indicate the soul's mortality — that it, too, comes and goes, and is no more? Transiency is written on the face of all things; why not on the soul? The last verse of the poem indicates that this is really the question which engages his thought. It indicates also, that, despite the fact of universal change, he will not believe it involves the soul's destruction.

"There rolls the deep where grew the tree.
  O earth, what changes hast thou seen !
  There where the long street roars hath been
The stillness of the central sea.

" The hills are shadows, and they flow
  From form to form, and nothing stands;
  They melt like mist, the solid lands,
 Like clouds they shape themselves and go.

" But in my spirit will I dwell,
  And dream my dream, and hold it true ;
  For tho' my lips may breathe adieu,
 I cannot think the thing farewell."

In poem cxxx., he reflects upon the Pantheistic doctrine of absorption into the Infinite after death. This doctrine is, of course, opposed to personal immortality. It cancels the individuality of the finite spirit by remergence "in the general soul." It is an interesting and rather singular thing to note, that a conception which Tennyson had previously emphatically rejected as —

  "faith as vague as all unsweet,"

affirming that the boundary lines of personality shall be preserved, that —

   "Eternal form shall still divide
    The Eternal Soul from all beside,
   And I shall know him when we meet," [1]

     [1] Poem XLVII.

should afterward be, at least, temporarily
accepted, as is manifest in this poem.
We cannot agree with Mr. Morton Luce,
that the poem must be interpreted from
the standpoint of poetic license. The
affirmations which it contains are too bold
and positive for that. Already in the
preceding poem he mingles "all the
world" with his friend; and here Arthur's
voice is affirmed to be "on the rolling
air;" he is heard "where the waters run;"
he is declared to be in the rising and setting sun; he seems to be felt as "some
diffusive power" "in star and flower;"
and, as though the identification with
"the All" is not sufficient, in the above
affirmations, he proceeds a step farther,
and declares his departed friend to be
"mixed with God and Nature." The
poem seems to be an expression of a
temporary mood or faith of the poet rather
than a licensed poetical expression. *Temporary faith*, it must be said, because it
does not reflect any permanent belief on

his part.   It is opposed to the general
tendency of his thought and belief, as we
have already seen, and as will be manifest
after further investigation. —

> " Thy voice is on the rolling air;
>   I hear thee where the waters run;
>   Thou standest in the rising sun,
> And in the setting thou art fair.

> " Where art thou then? I cannot guess;
>   But tho' I seem in star and flower
>   To feel thee some diffusive power,
> I do not therefore love thee less:

> " My love involves the love before;
>   My love is vaster passion now;
>   Tho' mixed with God and Nature thou,
> I seem to love thee more and more."

Immediately following the above canto
comes that superb declaration of his belief
in personal immortality, expressed in the
words : —

> " O living will that shalt endure
>   When all that seems shall suffer shock."

The reflective consideration of the
question of immortality, so far as *In Memoriam* is concerned, ends with the poem

quoted above, with the exception of the prologue, which, as previously stated, was probably one of the last written. Here we find another ground for belief presented. The poet, after considering the question for seventeen long years, breaks forth in a declaration of confidence that death does not end all, and bases this confidence on the justice of God. —

> " Thou madest Life in man and brute ;
>   Thou madest Death ; and lo, thy foot
> Is on the skull which thou hast made.

> " Thou wilt not leave us in the dust :
>   Thou madest man, he knows not why,
>   He thinks he was not made to die ;
> And thou hast made him : thou art just."

The full significance of these words can only be understood as we read them in the light of what he has said elsewhere on the same subject. In June, 1871, he wrote a letter of condolence to Mrs. Elmhirst, his friend from childhood, whose son had recently died. In it he says : " You cannot catch the voice, or feel the hands, or kiss the cheek, that is all; a separation for an hour, not an eternal farewell. If it were not so, that which made us would seem too cruel a Power to be worshipped, and could not be loved, but I trust you believe all this," [1] etc. In an extract from Queen Victoria's private Journal, dated Aug. 7, 1883, we have the same attitude indicated. We are told here that in conversation with Her Majesty, "he spoke with horror of the unbelievers and philosophers who would make you believe there was no other world, no Immortality, who tried to explain all away in a miserable manner. We agreed that were such a thing possible, God, who is Love, would be far more cruel than any human being." [2]

This prologue, coming at the end of his long struggle with doubt, is very refreshing indeed. There is a calm, dignified, but triumphant tone which shows that the poet has come out of the long conflict strengthened in faith. —

[1] Memoir, vol. ii., p. 105.   [2] Ibid. 457.

" Perplext in faith, but pure in deeds,
    At last he beat his music out."

" He fought his doubts and gather'd strength,
    He would not make his judgment blind,
    He faced the spectres of the mind
And laid them : thus he came at length

" To find a stronger faith his own."

Henceforth we find him more especially maintaining the Faith against the serious doubts of his age.

From *In Memoriam* we pass to the celebrated *Idylls of the King.*[1] Tennyson unfolds to us the real import of the *Idylls* in his words "To the Queen," which he appends to the poems : —

" accept this old imperfect tale,
New-old, and shadowing Sense at war with Soul."

These poems portray the conflict between the sensuous and the spiritual in man.

---

[1] There is a reference to immortality in *Maud*, pt. i., sec. xviii., div. 7. Mr. Luce interprets the words as follows : " The thought appears to be twofold : 1st, ' The approach of death should make us dearer to each other ; ' 2nd, ' But death is immortality, and immortality alone can make love perfect.' " — *A Handbook to the Works of Alfred Lord Tennyson*, p. 316, n.

The bearing of the *Idylls* on the subject under consideration is seen in the words of the King, at the close of *The Holy Grail.* He tells his knights what are the duties of the King; and then of the visions which arise after those duties have been performed. These visions take him beyond the world of sense into the spiritual realm, — the world of the real. Here the spirit comes in contact with itself, with its Spiritual Cause, and with its spiritual destiny. It perceives itself as *actual,* rather than phenomenal. It perceives God as *Reality,* rather than as vision. It apprehends itself not "as a thing that dies," but as a being immortal. The King speaks: —

> " ' And some among you held, that if the King
> Had seen the sight he would have sworn the vow :
> Not easily, seeing that the King must guard
> That which he rules, and is but as the hind
> To whom a space of land is given to plow.
> Who may not wander from the allotted field
> Before his work be done ; but, being done,
> Let visions of the night or of the day

Come, as they will; and many a time they come,
Until this earth he walks on seems not earth,
This light that strikes his eyeball is not light,
This air that smites his forehead is not air
But vision — yea, his very hand and foot —
In moments when he feels he cannot die,
And knows himself no vision to himself,
Nor the high God a vision, nor that One
Who rose again.'"

Has Tennyson, in all of the superb crea-
tions of his genius, ever given us anything
finer than this? These are the lines
which he pronounced "the (spiritually)
central lines of the *Idylls;*"[1] and, so far
as they bear on our subject, they declare
that there are supreme moments in the
life of the soul when it intuits its own
immortality, — moments when it feels itself to be not a perishable, temporal thing,
but an imperishable, immortal spirit;
moments when it *feels it cannot die.*

Passing from the *Idylls* to the volume
entitled *Tiresias, and other Poems,*[2] we

[1] Memoir, vol. ii., p. 90.
[2] Published 1885. The volume entitled *Ballads,
and other Poems*, published 1880, has several refer-

meet with a poem, — *The Charge of the Heavy Brigade at Balaclava.*[1] In the *Epilogue* there is a positive declaration of Tennyson's belief in immortality, with a semi-argumentative presentation of the same. He affirms the vanity of deed and song, if man be not immortal; and that man's moral achievements will continue as a moulding force in the life after death. The *Epilogue* is a poem favoring peace rather than war. It represents a conversation between Irene (Greek word for Peace) and a poet. Irene tells the poet that he will never set his name —

" A star among the stars,"

by praising that which should be blamed, namely, " The barbarism of wars." The poet replies that he has been misunderstood. He wants wars to cease. He merely contends that it is right to crown

ences to immortality. However, they are not important for our purpose. They occur in *Rizpah*, *The Sisters*, *Dedicatory Poem to the Princess Alice*, and *De Profundis*.

[1] First published in *Macmillan's Magazine*, 1881.

the warrior's noble deeds with song.   He
hopes the crown may last, but affirms that—

> " Song will vanish in the vast."

Irene objects to this affirmation, and the
poet yields to the objection, modifying
his previous statement by saying, that
"deed and song" will pass away and be
in vain, unless "man himself remain."
And, says the poet, remain he will, and
so will his moral achievement, serving to
mould him in the life beyond the grave.—

> " Let it live then — ay, till when?
>   Earth passes, all is lost
> In what they prophesy, our wise men,
>   Sun-flame or sunless frost,
> And deed and song alike are swept
>   Away, and all in vain
> As far as man can see, except
>   The man himself remain ;
> And tho', in this lean age forlorn,
>   Too many a voice may cry
> That man can have no after-morn,
>   Not yet of these am I.
> The man remains, and whatsoe'er
>   He wrought of good or brave
> Will mould him thro' the cycle-year
>   That dawns behind the grave."

If, in the next place, we turn to *Tiresias*, we find Tennyson, in the Epilogue, postulating immortality on the ground of the uselessness of life, if man be not immortal. In 1883, Tennyson sent this poem, "dating many years ago," to Edward Fitzgerald,[1] an old friend. It was found by his son Hallam "in some forgotten book" of the poet. It was published in the volume of 1885, already referred to. The Epilogue is very touching. It refers to the death of Fitzgerald, or "old Fitz," as Tennyson fondly called him. Referring pathetically to their friendship, he says, —

"Gone into darkness, that full light
    Of friendship! past, in sleep, away
By night, into the deeper night!
    The deeper night? A clearer day
Than our poor twilight dawn on earth —
    If night, what barren toil to be!
What life, so maim'd by night, were worth
    Our living out? Not mine to me
Remembering all the golden hours
    Now silent, and so many dead,
And him the last."

[1] The translator of the *Rubaiyat of Omar Khayyam.*

In this volume of 1885 is contained also *The Ancient Sage*. The nature of this speculative poem has already been explained, and a partial analysis of it given so far as it bears on the problem of the being and nature of God. But the poem also deals with the question of immortality. The agnostic and materialistic youth presents his views on this subject in the "scroll of verse," and the sage replies to them. In our previous analysis we had reached the point where the youth recognises no other Deity than Time, and he proceeds to call attention to its destructive power, insinuating that eventually man must succumb to it and be no more. He presents, in a very forcible manner, the argument of change, as manifest in the gradual decline of man's powers : —

> " ' The statesman's brain that sway'd the past.
>   Is feebler than his knees ;
>   The passive sailor wrecks at last
>   In ever-silent seas;

The warrior hath forgot his arms,
    The Learned all his lore ;
The changing market frets or charms
    The merchant's hope no more;
The prophet's beacon burn'd in vain,
    And now is lost in cloud ;
The plowman passes, bent with pain,
    To mix with what he plow'd ;
The poet whom his Age would quote
    As heir of endless fame—
He knows not ev'n the book he wrote,
    Not even his own name.
For man has overlived his day,
    And darkening in the light,
Scarce feels the senses break away
    To mix with ancient Night.' "

But, says the sage in reply, —

" The shell must break before the bird can fly."

The decline and dissolution of the body
merely liberate the spirit. But the
youth in the scroll continues :—

    " ' The years that when my Youth began
        Had set the lily and rose
    By all my ways where'er they ran,
        Have ended mortal foes ;
    My rose of love for ever gone,
        My lily of truth and trust —

They made her lily and rose in one,
   And changed her into dust.
O rose tree planted in my grief,
   And growing, on her tomb,
Her dust is greening in your leaf,
   Her blood is in your bloom.
O slender lily waving there,
   And laughing back the light,
In vain you tell me " Earth is fair "
   When all is dark as night.' "

But, says the sage, this is a misinterpretation of the work of Time. Man is immortal, and awaits "the second state sublime," when he can view this work of Time from the standpoint of "the last and largest sense." This sense will reveal to him the true interpretation, — "that the world is wholly fair."

" My son, the world is dark with griefs and graves,
So dark that men cry out against the Heavens.
Who knows but that the darkness is in man?
The doors of Night may be the gates of Light;
For wert thou born or blind or deaf, and then
Suddenly heal'd, how would'st thou glory in all
The splendours and the voices of the world !
And we, the poor earth's dying race, and yet
No phantoms, watching from a phantom shore,

Await the last and largest sense to make
The phantom walls of this illusion fade,
And show us that the world is wholly fair."

Perusing the scroll again, the sage finds
it still affirming the mortality of man:

" For all that laugh, and all that weep
    And all that breathe are one
  Slight ripple on the boundless deep
    That moves, and all is gone."

But, says the sage, in reply, man is
conscious of his immortality in his very
relation to this "boundless deep."

" But that one ripple on the boundless deep
  Feels that the deep is boundless, and itself
  For ever changing form, but evermore
  One with the boundless motion of the deep."

And, at the suggestion of the scroll, that
"the darkness of the pall" should be forgotten in wine and golden music, the
sage takes occasion to remark, that not
only the darkness associated with life, but
also that associated with death is a misinterpretation. There are stars that shine
in the night. There are some, too, that

never set, but pass beyond the range of
mortal vision "to lose themselves in day."
There is a happier and worthier view of
death. "The dead are not dead." They
live, and their lot is a higher and happier
one than ours. Therefore, they should
be borne "to burial or to burning," not
on the black bier which stands for nega-
tion, but in white, —

"With songs in praise of death, and crown'd with
     flowers !" [1]

But there is continued affirmation in
the scroll of man's mortality.

"O worms and maggots of to-day
   Without their hope of wings!"

  .   .   .   .   .

"Tho' some have gleams or so they say
   Of more than mortal things."

The sage confesses himself to be one of
those who have had such "gleams."
They have given him an insight into that
which lies beyond "the gates of birth and

[1] It would be difficult to find anything more hopeful
and cheerful than this in all literature.

death." Pre-existence and immortality
have been revealed to him by these
"gleams." Of the gleams of the immortal life he says: —

> " for more than once when I
> Sat all alone, revolving in myself
> The word that is the symbol of myself,
> The mortal limit of the Self was loosed,
> And past into the Nameless, as a cloud
> Melts into Heaven. I touch'd my limbs, the
>   limbs
> Were strange not mine — and yet no shade of
>   doubt,
> But utter clearness, and thro' loss of Self
> The gain of such large life as match'd with ours
> Were Sun to spark — unshadowable in words,
> Themselves but shadows of a shadow-world."

Tennyson here, in the reply of the sage,
is referring to a personal experience
which constituted for him a ground for
believing in the soul's immortality. It
was a trance experience which was not
uncommon with him. He refers to it in
the ninety-fifth poem of *In Memoriam*.
In the experience there described he was
brought into contact with the spirit of

the dead.   He came face to face also with
the real — the Eternal — and had a profound sense of his own immortality.   He

> "came on that which is, and caught
> The deep pulsations of the world,"

> "Æonian music measuring out
> The steps of Time — the shocks of Chance
> The blows of Death."

In the description given in *The Ancient
Sage*, he tells us that —

> "The mortal limit of the self was loosed," —

and he entered upon —

> "such large life as match'd with ours
> Were Sun to spark."

We have still another description of
this trance experience in words of Tennyson recorded in the *Memoir:* [1] "A kind of
waking trance I have frequently had, quite
up from boyhood, when I have been all
alone.   This has generally come upon
me thro' repeating my own name two or
three times to myself silently, till all at

[1] Vol. i., p. 320.

once, as it were out of the intensity of the
consciousness of individuality, the individuality itself seemed to dissolve and
fade away into boundless being, and this
not a confused state, but the clearest of
the clearest, the surest of the surest, the
weirdest of the weirdest, utterly beyond
words, where death was an almost laugh-
able impossibility, the loss of personality
(if so it were) seemed no extinction but
the only true life." [1]

These "gleams" of pre-existence and
immortality, these gleams "of more than
mortal things," are merely "idle gleams"
to the youth, as the scroll reveals. They
are transient "but the clouds remain."
But what are idle gleams to the youth are
"light" to the sage; and he urges the
youth to forsake the life of the flesh — the
lower life of selfishness — which clouds
the spiritual vision; and enjoins him to
enter upon the moral life — the higher life
of service to self and others; then, climb-

---

[1] This is a close approach to Pantheism.

ing the Mount of Blessing, perchance he may catch a glimpse of immortality, he may see, "past the range of Night and Shadow," —

> " The high-heaven dawn of more than mortal day
> Strike on the Mount of Vision ! "

In *Locksley Hall Sixty Years After*,[1] there is a fine passage expressing Tennyson's faith in immortality, with more or less of a justification of it. He calls it "the leading light of man." He comments on the universality of the belief; and finally affirms that such noble traits of human character as goodness, truth, purity, and justice "crumble into dust," if we rob them of immortality. —

> " Truth, for Truth is Truth, he worshipt, being
> true as he was brave ;
> Good, for Good is Good, he follow'd, yet he
> look'd beyond the grave,[2]

[1] Probably written shortly before 1886, and published in the volume, *Locksley Hall Sixty Years After, and other Poems*, 1886.   Dated 1887.

[2] Probably descriptive of his son Lionel. Cf. Memoir, vol. ii., p. 329.

" Wiser there than you, that crowning barren
      Death as lord of all,
Deem this over-tragic drama's closing curtain is
      the pall !

" Beautiful was death in him, who saw the death,
      but kept the deck,
Saving women and their babes, and sinking with
      the sinking wreck,

" Gone for ever !   Ever ? no — for since our dying
      race began,
Ever, ever, and for ever was the leading light of
      man.

" Those that in barbarian burials kill'd the slave,
      and slew the wife
Felt within themselves the sacred passion of the
      second life.

" Indian warriors dream of ampler hunting grounds
      beyond the night ;
Ev'n the black Australian dying hopes he shall
      return, a white.

" Truth for truth, and good for good ! The Good,
      the True, the Pure, the Just —
Take the charm ' For ever ' from them, and they
      crumble into dust."

And one of the last couplets of this poem
embodies the injunction : —

" Follow Light, and do the Right — for man can
        half-control his doom —
    Till you find the deathless Angel seated in the
        vacant tomb."

On Dec. 13, 1889, when Tennyson
was eighty years old, appeared his volume
entitled *Demeter and other Poems*. There
are several poems in this volume which
merely indicate Tennyson's belief in
immortality, such as *The Ring*, and *By an
Evolutionist*. But there is one which is
of great interest as marking probably the
close of this third stage or moment in the
development of his thought on immortality,
— the period of rational consideration.
The poem is entitled *Vastness*. It is a
most emphatic reiteration of a " reason "
for belief in the future life which was very
influential with Tennyson. This reason
or ground of belief is the absolute vanity,
the utter uselessness and meaningless-
ness of all things if man be not immortal.   Politics, stately purposes, valor in
battle, glorious annals, martyrdom for the

right, pain and pleasure, wealth and pov-
erty, fame and love, the loss of the flesh
and the conquest of the spirit; spring
and summer, autumn and winter; old and
new-old revolutions; philosophies and
sciences; poetry and prayer, — what do all
these things amount to, what meaning do
they have, what purpose do they serve, —

"if we all of us end but in being our
own corpse-coffins at last,
Swallow'd in Vastness, lost in Silence, drown'd in
the deeps of a meaningless Past?

"What but a murmur of gnats in the gloom, or a
moment's anger of bees in their hive?"

If man's end is the grave, then, indeed,
are vanity and worthlessness written on
the face of all things human.   Nothing is
more apparent to the poet than this, and
it seems as though, after a long period of
argument with himself and his age, he
means to close the discussion with an
emphatic re-statement of the fact, and an
affirmation, that "the dead are not dead,
but alive."

Thus, in this long stretch of years, extending from 1833 to 1889, — covering fifty-six years of the poet's life, — do we find him earnestly reflecting on the question of human destiny. During this long period the question receives rational consideration, — the evidence for and against belief in immortality being carefully weighed. Sometimes he rests in the favorable evidence as though he had reached a permanent attitude. Then, such evidence seems to lose its force, and the opposing evidence rests heavily upon his mind. Sometimes reason catches a glimpse of "more than mortal day." Again, it is enveloped in the darkness of everlasting night.

During this period he has fully considered the argument from sense. The dead man's face indicates naught of "passion, pain, or pride." Calm indifference to all things cosmic and human is his state. The poet has seen change and decay written on the face of Nature. Things come and go. Nothing abides. Man's body returns to the dust. Yea, even his mental powers decline and ultimately fail. Transiency is the law of all things — minds included.

During this period he has also considered the claims of Scepticism. All things finite have had a beginning and must therefore have an end. "To begin implies to end." Genesis involves Nemesis. Man is no exception to the rule. He also has had a beginning. To affirm his pre-existence is to talk of dreams. He, therefore, falls under the law. His extinction is involved in his generation.

This period also reveals the poet considering the claims of Materialism. All so-called psychic phenomena are nothing more than higher forms of neural motion. Man is "wholly brain," and as such, is so completely identified with Nature as to be her product. Like all physical things, then, he is subject to change and dissolution. Being merely a "cunning cast in clay," he ultimately breaks and returns to earth. The poet has questioned Nature on this point and has found her answer to be in harmony with these claims. Her only reply is : —

> " I bring to life, I bring to death :
> The spirit does but mean the breath :
> I know no more."

During this period he has also dwelt on the claims of Pantheism. Man, after all, has but a phenomenal existence. He is merely a mode of the activity of the Absolute. He seems to have a being of his own; but it is no more distinct from the being of the Absolute than is the being of the wave or billow from that of the sea. At death this particular mode of the Absolute's being is cancelled. The billow loses its apparent individuality by being absorbed by the sea. So man loses his apparent reality by being "mixed with God and Nature," or by "remergence in the general soul." He is absorbed by and into the Infinite. Hence there is no personal immortality.

And finally, during this period, he also considered the claims of Agnosticism. There are limits to man's knowledge. These limits are constitutional — imposed on him by the constitution of mind itself. Knowledge is limited to the phenomenal; it does not extend to the noumenal. The soul and its immortality belong to the latter realm. Because of mental impotency, then, man is shut out from a knowledge of his own immortality. We cannot know. This is the only true and becoming attitude for man to take toward this great question.

On the other hand, the poet, during this long period, has considered also the evidence in favor of belief in immortality. Very early in this period he set the "inward evidence" of spirit over against the outward evidence of sense: —

1. Man aspires after a nobler destiny than the dust. He sits, "shaping wings

to fly." There are forebodings of a mystery in his heart. The name Eternity is upon his lips.

2. Man is a religious, rational, and moral being. Does not an investiture of this character link him to the supernatural and make him an heir of immortality? A being so divine in nature — who has the conception of a God and of his relation to him; who reasons about a beginning and an end; who distinguishes between right and wrong, and is conscious of moral obligation, — such a being cannot perish with the body.

3. Once more, man has peculiar intimations of his immortality.—

> "Heaven opens inward, chasms yawn,
>   Vast images in glimmering dawn,
>   Half shown, are broken and withdrawn."

4. Again, the very fact that man doubts his own mortality in spite of the evidence to the contrary, constitutes a pre-supposition in its favor. At least, it destroys the force of the unbeliever's

argument, for he is slain by his own weapon, which is doubt.

5. And, finally, man does not long for death, — absolute extinction. What he wants is life, — a larger, fuller, richer, completer life. Why should not this supreme yearning of the soul be satisfied?

But the poet does not rest in this evidence. A little later he considers other "reasons" for belief : —

6. Life itself should teach us that if man is not immortal, then earth to its innermost centre is darkness, — an absolutely unintelligible reality, — possessing no meaning whatever. This implies a Godless world and the destruction of all religious ideals; for, under such circumstances, what does *God* mean to the human soul?

7. Again, life would lose its significance on the basis of such a supposition. It would be worthless — not worth the living. Indeed, 't were better to cease to be at once.

8. Again, love, the supreme emotion of the human heart, were an impossibility on such an hypothesis. Or, if possible, it could scarcely rise above the sensual passion of the brute.

9. Again, not only does man's superiority of endowment argue his immortality, as already pointed out, but the glory and worth of his character and achievement really entitle him to it. Does not a being who worships God under adverse circumstances, who trusts God as Love, and Love as "Creation's final law," despite the cruel and bloody course of nature, deserve immortality? Does not a being who reveals "splendid purpose," who loves, who suffers, who battles for lofty ideals, — "the True, the Right," — deserve a nobler destiny than to —

> "Be blown about the desert dust,
> Or seal'd within the iron hills?"

If not, then this being is "a monster," "a dream," "a discord," and his life is as "futile" as it is "frail."

10. Again, the great cosmic process indicates man's immortality. It does this in two ways: (*a*) Evolution is the order of the world's on-going. Progress from the lower to the higher seems to be the cosmic order of procedure. Man himself is involved in this cosmic order. Hence he, too, moves from a lower to a higher state. True to this order of the universe, he is "the herald of himself in higher place." But (*b*) man stands at the head of creation. He is Nature's supreme work. All of her work preceding the coming of man was preparatory to his advent. In view of this stupendous preparation, man must have a greater career than is implied in threescore years and ten. He must "breathe an ampler day" than this, "for ever nobler ends."

11. Again, Justice is a fundamental attribute of Deity. To create a being who desires immortality, who yearns for life, — higher, richer, completer life, — and then fail to satisfy his yearning, is

irreconcilable with God's justice. To
cancel such a being's existence is out of
all harmony with the essential nature of
God.

12. Again, there are times when the
soul intuits its own immortality. They
come with the consciousness of duty performed. They are the supreme moments
in the life of the spirit, when it stands
face to face with reality — with the reality of God; with the reality of self; with
the reality of its own immortality. Moments when man —

> "feels he cannot die,
> And knows himself no vision to himself,
> Nor the high God a vision."

13. Again, the belief in man's immortality is not only universal, but it is also
the essential condition of human progress.
There are certain fundamental virtues
which lie at the foundations of all social
order and condition its progress. These
are Goodness, Truth, Purity, and Justice.
They are human attributes. Were we to

rob them of immortality, they would "crumble into dust."

14. Again, there are super-normal experiences in the life of the soul which throw light on this great question, — experiences when "the mortal limit of the Self" is loosed and the soul is carried "beyond the gates of birth and death." To one who has had such experiences, the claims of mortality seem absurd. In such a trance there is a —

> "gain of such large life as match'd with ours
> Were Sun to spark — unshadowable in words."

These are the considerations which make for belief in immortality. They are the reasons for faith which Tennyson gave to himself and to others during fifty-six years of serious reflection. He did not present them as constituting a *proof* or *demonstration* of the soul's immortality. He believed rather that immortality, like God and freedom, belonged to —

> "The truths that never can be proved
>   Until we close with all we loved,
> And all we flow from, soul in soul."

Indeed, at one time he did not regard
some, at least, of the above "reasons"
as closing "grave doubts and answers,"
but as merely the work of sorrow, whose
"care is not to part and prove," making
doubt subservient to love, loosing —

> "from the lip
> Short swallow-flights of song, that dip
> Their wings in tears, and skim away."

He says emphatically in *The Ancient
Sage* —

> "Thou canst not prove thou art immortal, no
> Nor yet that thou art mortal."

Immortality is neither a truth of sense
nor of understanding, but of faith, wherefore we are enjoined to "cling to Faith."
But this faith is a *rational*, not a *blind*
faith. It is based on reason; and Tennyson, during these fifty years and more,
has been trying "to give a reason for the
faith," — to unfold its rational character
— with the results recorded above. It
is evident, then, that he takes the same
attitude toward immortality that he takes

toward God and freedom, viz. : that it is not a truth of knowledge, but of faith.

And this brings us to the fourth period in the history of Tennyson's attitude toward this vital question. This is the attitude of comparatively undisturbed repose in the belief in man's immortality. He has fought his own doubts and the doubts of his age for more than half a century. He has gained the victory over personal doubt and has done valiant service in defence of the Faith. He is now at peace. This is already manifest in *Demeter and other Poems*, especially in the beautiful lyric, *Crossing the Bar,* embodying a more beautiful faith.[1] For him, as revealed by this poem, the grave

[1] Tennyson's son says: "'Crossing the Bar' was written in my father's eighty-first year, on a day in October when we came from Aldworth to Farringford. Before reaching Farringford he had the Moaning of the Bar in his mind, and after dinner he showed me this poem written out.

"I said, 'That is the crown of your life's work.' He answered, 'It came in a moment.' He explained the 'Pilot' as 'That Divine and Unseen who is always guiding us.'"— Memoir, vol. ii. pp. 366, 367.

has lost its victory and death has lost its sting. The poet wants "no sadness of farewell" when he embarks upon the sea whose flood may bear him far "from out our bourne of Time and Place;" because, he says, —

> "I hope to see my Pilot face to face
> When I have crost the bar."

Death is merely "that which drew from out the boundless deep," turning home again.

This calm and peaceful faith is further manifest in the last volume of his poems, entitled, *The Death of Œnone, Akbar's Dream, and other Poems.* This volume was published a few weeks after his death, which occurred Oct. 16, 1892. Here we meet with the poem entitled *Faith*, which is undoubtedly expressive of the faith of the poet. Death will fling open "the gates that bar the distance," and the immortal life will bring with it worthier conceptions of the character of

God than those expressed by human creeds.
Even here there "comes a gleam of what
is higher."

> " Neither mourn if human creeds be lower than the
>   heart's desire !
>   Thro' the gates that bar the distance comes a
>   gleam of what is higher.
>   Wait till Death has flung them open, when the
>   man will make the Maker
>   Dark no more with human hatreds in the glare of
>   deathless fire ! "

Here, too, there is the little poem, *The
Silent Voices*, which reveals his thought
as pushing forward into the future life.
There is almost an impatient yearning to
enter into its realities. He cares more
for "the heights beyond" than for "the
lowland ways behind."

> "When the dumb Hour, clothed in black,
>   Brings the Dreams about my bed,
>   Call me not so often back,
>   Silent Voices of the dead,
>   Toward the lowland ways behind me,
>   And the sunlight that is gone !
>   Call me rather, silent voices,

Forward to the starry track
Glimmering up the heights beyond me
On, and always on ! "

Again, in the poem entitled, *God and the Universe*, he reveals a calm and dignified faith.   His son informs us, that several hours before his father's death he exclaimed, "I have opened it."   The son adds: "whether this referred to the Shakespeare opened by him at

'Hang there like fruit, my soul,
Till the tree die,'

which he always called among the tenderest lines in Shakespeare : or whether one of his last poems, of which he was fond, was running through his head I cannot tell "[1]   *God and the Universe* is the poem referred to.   After asking, —

" Will my tiny spark of being wholly vanish in
your deeps and heights ?
Must my day be dark by reason, O ye Heavens,
of your boundless nights,
Rush of Suns, and roll of systems, and your fiery
clash of meteorites ? "

[1] Memoir, vol. ii. pp. 427, 428.

he answers : —

> "Spirit, nearing yon dark portal at the limit of thy
>   human state,
> Fear not thou the hidden purpose of that Power
>   which alone is great,
> Nor the myriad world, His shadow, nor the Silent
>   Opener of the Gate."

And, finally, in *The Death of the Duke of Clarence and Avondale*, we have a splendid declaration of the poet's faith in the words : —

> "The face of Death is toward the Sun of Life,
> His shadow darkens earth : his truer name
> Is 'Onward,' no discordance in the roll
> And march of that Eternal Harmony
> Whereto the worlds beat time, tho' faintly heard
> Until the great Hereafter."

Thus, in all of these poems, he strikes a clear note. There is no wavering of faith. It remains sure and steadfast. His own doubts have vanished. He has sailed "the sunless gulfs of doubt" of his age and has issued into a sunlit sea of faith. For him, "utter darkness" does not close the day. Far out beyond

" A hundred ever-rising mountain lines,
   And past the range of Night and Shadow "

he sees —

   " The high-heaven dawn of more than mortal day
   Strike on the Mount of Vision ! "

Is it any wonder, after such a long period of earnest consideration of the question of immortality, culminating in such a serene personal faith, that the poet, a few days before his death, should make the request of his son, " Mind you put ' Crossing the Bar ' at the end of all editions of my poems "?[1] Is not his meaning clear? Is not the request a communication to the world of his belief in the " life everlasting "? And how surpassingly beautiful is the belief which is expressed, as well as the manner of its expression ! —

" Sunset and evening star,
   And one clear call for me !
And may there be no moaning of the bar,
   When I put out to sea,

[1] Memoir, vol. ii. p. 367.

" But such a tide as moving seems asleep,
　　Too full for sound and foam,
　When that which drew from out the boundless
　　　deep
　　Turns again home.

" Twilight and evening bell,
　　And after that the dark !
　And may there be no sadness of farewell,
　　When I embark ;

" For tho' from out our bourne of Time and Place
　　The flood may bear me far,
　I hope to see my Pilot face to face
　　When I have crost the bar."

INDEX